AF404705

CBSE Term II 2022

Information Technology

(Code 402)

Class X

Complete Theory in Sync with Syllabus | Case Based Questions | Short/Long Answer Questions | 3 Practice Papers with Explanations

Author
Rashi Bansal

arihant
ARIHANT PRAKASHAN (School Division Series)

CBSE Term II
2022

arihant

ARIHANT PRAKASHAN (School Division Series)

卐 **Administrative & Production Offices**

Regd. Office
'Ramchhaya' 4577/15, Agarwal Road, Darya Ganj, New Delhi -110002
Tele: 011- 47630600, 43518550

卐 **Head Office**
Kalindi, TP Nagar, Meerut (UP) - 250002, Tel: 0121-7156203, 7156204

卐 **Sales & Support Offices**
Agra, Ahmedabad, Bengaluru, Bareilly, Chennai, Delhi, Guwahati, Hyderabad, Jaipur, Jhansi, Kolkata, Lucknow, Nagpur & Pune.

卐 **ISBN :** 978-93-25796-69-0

卐 **PRICE :** ₹125.00

PO No : TXT-XX-XXXXXXX-X-XX

Published by Arihant Publications (India) Ltd.

For further information about the books published by Arihant, log on to www.arihantbooks.com or e-mail at info@arihantbooks.com

Follow us on

Contents

Syllabus

CBSE Term II Class X

Part A	Employability Skills	Mark
Unit 4	Entrepreneurial Skills-II	05
Unit 5	Green Skills-II	
	Total	**05**
Part B	**Subject Specific Skills**	**Marks**
Unit 3	Database Management System	10
Unit 4	Web Applications and Security	10
	Total	**20**
	Grand Total	**25 Marks**

CBSE Circular

Acad - 51/2021, 05 July 2021

Exam Scheme Term I & II

केन्द्रीय माध्यमिक शिक्षा बोर्ड

(शिक्षा मंत्रालय, भारत सरकार के अधीन एक स्वायत संगठन)

CENTRAL BOARD OF SECONDARY EDUCATION

(An Autonomous Organisation under the Ministryof Education, Govt. of India)

Term I Examinations:

- At the end of the first term, the Board will organize **Term I Examination** in a flexible schedule to be conducted between November-December 2021 with a window period of 4-8 weeks for schools situated in different parts of country and abroad. Dates for conduct of examinations will be notified subsequently.
- The Question Paper will have Multiple Choice Questions (MCQ) including case-based MCQs and MCQs on assertion-reasoning type. Duration of test will be **90 minutes** and it will cover only the rationalized syllabus of **Term I only** (i.e. approx. 50% of the entire syllabus).
- Question Papers will be sent by the CBSE to schools along with marking scheme.
- The exams will be conducted under the supervision of the External Center Superintendents and Observers appointed by CBSE.
- The responses of students will be captured on OMR sheets which, after scanning may be directly uploaded at CBSE portal or alternatively may be evaluated and marks obtained will be uploaded by the school on the very same day. The final direction in this regard will be conveyed to schools by the Examination Unit of the Board.
- Marks of the **Term I** Examination will contribute to the final overall score of students.

Term II Examination/ Year-end Examination:

- At the end of the second term, the Board would organize **Term II or Year-end Examination** based on the rationalized syllabus of Term II only (i.e. approximately 50% of the entire syllabus).
- This examination would be held around **March-April 2022** at the examination centres fixed by the Board.
- The paper will be of **2 hours duration** and have questions of different formats (case-based/ situation based, open ended- short answer/ long answer type).
- In case the situation is not conducive for normal descriptive examination **a 90 minute MCQ based exam** will be conducted at the end of the Term II also.
- Marks of the Term II Examination would contribute to the final overall score.

To cover this situation, we have given both MCQs and Subjective Questions in each Chapter.

केन्द्रीय माध्यमिक शिक्षा बोर्ड

(शिक्षा मंत्रालय, भारत सरकार के अधीन एक स्वायत संगठन)

CENTRAL BOARD OF SECONDARY EDUCATION

(An Autonomous Organisation under the Ministryof Education, Govt. of India)

Assessment / Examination as per different situations

A. In case the situation of the pandemic improves and students are able to come to schools or centres for taking the exams.

Board would conduct Term I and Term II examinations at schools/centres and the theory marks will be distributed equally between the two exams.

B. In case the situation of the pandemic forces complete closure of schools during November-December 2021, but Term II exams are held at schools or centres.

Term I MCQ based examination would be done by students online/offline from home - in this case, the weightage of this exam for the final score would be reduced, and weightage of Term II exams will be increased for declaration of final result.

C. In case the situation of the pandemic forces complete closure of schools during March-April 2022, but Term I exams are held at schools or centres.

Results would be based on the performance of students on Term I MCQ based examination and internal assessments. The weightage of marks of Term I examination conducted by the Board will be increased to provide year end results of candidates.

D. In case the situation of the pandemic forces complete closure of schools and Board conducted Term I and II exams are taken by the candidates from home in the session 2021-22.

Results would be computed on the basis of the Internal Assessment/Practical/Project Work and Theory marks of Term-I and II exams taken by the candidate from home in Class X / XII subject to the moderation or other measures to ensure validity and reliability of the assessment.

In all the above cases, data analysis of marks of students will be undertaken to ensure the integrity of internal assessments and home based exams.

Dr. Joseph Emmanuel
Director (Academics)

CHAPTER 01

Entrepreneurial Skills-II

In this Chapter...

- Entrepreneur
- Qualities/ Characteristics of a Good Entrepreneur
- Functions of an Entrepreneur
- Role and Significance/Importance of Entrepreneur
- Myths of Entrepreneurship
- Advantages of Entrepreneurship
- Disadvantages of Entrepreneurship

Entrepreneur

The word 'entrepreneur' is derived from the French word 'entrepreneur' which means to undertake. An entrepreneur is an individual who creates a new business, bearing most of the risks and enjoying most of the rewards.

Howard W. Johnson was an American educator. He says entrepreneur is composite of three basic elements (i) invention, (ii) innovation and (iii) adaptation.

According to Joseph Schumpeter, "Entrepreneurs as innovators, who use the process of entrepreneurship to shatter the status quo of the existing products and services, to set new products, new services."

Entrepreneurship and Society

An entrepreneur has some personal qualities which influence his behaviour. No doubt, he lives in a society and therefore economic opportunities and gains affect him. Entrepreneur creates organisations. Entrepreneurship is affected by economic opportunities and gains as the entrepreneur lives in a society. Entrepreneurs promote investment, increase in production bring competitiveness in business, reduce costs of products and raise the standard of living in society.

Qualities/Characteristics of a Good Entrepreneur

The major qualities/characteristics of a good entrepreneur are linked below

- **Leadership** An entrepreneur must possess the characteristics of leadership and must lead a team for achievement of goals. The leader is able to clearly articulate their ideas and has a clear vision. An entrepreneurial leader realises the importance of initiative and reactiveness and they go out of their way to provide a support to the team.
- **Risk Taking** An entrepreneur with rational planning and firm decisions bear the risks. They have differentiated approach towards risks. Good entrepreneurs are always ready to invest their time and money but they always have a back up for every risk they take.
- **Innovativeness** With the changing needs and requirements of customers production should meet requirements with the help of innovative ideas. An entrepreneurial venture does not have to restrict itself to just one innovation or even one type of innovation. Success can be built on combination of innovation. *For example*, a new product delivered in a new way with a new message.

- **Goal-oriented** Goal-oriented entrepreneurs achieve the maximum results from their efforts in business due to the fact they work towards clear and measurable targets.
- **Decision-maker** An entrepreneur has to take many decisions to put his business idea into reality. He chooses the best suitable and profitable alternative.
- **Highly Optimistic** A successful entrepreneur is always optimistic and the present problems does not matter to them. He is always hopeful that the situation will became favourable for business in future.
- **Motivator** An entrepreneur has to create a spirit of team work and motivate them. So that he gets full cooperation from the employees.
- **Self-confident** An entrepreneur should have confidence to achieve his goals otherwise he won't be able to convince his team to achieve his goals.
- **Action-oriented** An entrepreneur should have an action oriented vision and ideology to plan things well.
- **Dynamic Agent** An entrepreneur creates new needs and new means to satisfy them. He has the ability to visualise new ventures and new plans.
- **High Achiever** An entrepreneurs are high achievers as they have a strong urge to achieve. The most important characteristic is his achievement motivation.
- **Trust in Self** An entrepreneur believes on their own decisions and actions as he has trust in his perseverance and creations. He does not believe in luck.

Functions of an Entrepreneur

The various functions of an entrepreneur may be classified and described as under

- **Innovation** It includes introducing new products, opening new markets, new sources of raw material and new organisation structure.
- **Risk Taking** An entrepreneur has to take risk by choosing one among various alternatives.
- **Decision-making** It includes stabilising organisation's aims and objectives and changing them according to changing conditions, taking decisions on effective techniques, utilisation of financial resources etc. So, decision-making is an important function of an entrepreneur.
- **Organisation and Management** An entrepreneur organise and manage various economic and human factors through planning, coordination, control, supervision and direction.
- **Size and Scale of Business Unit** An entrepreneur has to decide about the size of business unit as he wants to establish one production unit or more dependent upon the demand of the product. Similarly, he has to decide about scale of production i.e. small scale, middle scale or large scale.
- **Appointment of Managerial and Other Work Force** It is the entrepreneur who appoints the management staff as well as other work force as per the requirement and needs of the enterprise.
- **Factors of Production** The factors of production i.e. land, labour, capital etc., should be in appropriate proportion and to maximise output of these factors is the responsibility of the entrepreneur.
- **Control and Direction** He must exercise control over all departments and direct them on a timely basis.
- **Finding Suitable Market** A proper research must be done to find a suitable market for selling the products. Other functions like advertisement and publicity, appointment of selling agents, providing incentives to various selling intermediaries to promote sales should be given priority.
- **New Inventions and Innovations** New inventions and innovations must be encouraged and introduced in production, sales, marketing, advertisement etc.
- **Establishing Relations with Government** An entrepreneur must establish good relations with government and its functionaries. His functions are to obtain licences, payment of taxes, selling the product to government, provision for export-import etc.
- **Establishing Contacts with Competitors** An entrepreneur must form contacts with the competitors to analyse the market. He must be in a position to make opportunities out of the given situation.

Role and Significance/Importance of Entrepreneur

An entrepreneur is the builder of economic growth. He promotes the prosperity of a country by his initiative and skill for innovation and dynamic leadership. He creates wealth, opens up employment opportunities and fosters the other segments of economic system.

The role and significance of an entrepreneur are given under the following headings

- **Organiser of Society's Productive Resources** An entrepreneur is the organiser of society's productive resources. He is the person who assembles the unused natural, physical and human resources of the society, combines them properly, establishes effective coordination between them and makes the economic activities dynamic.
- **Helpful in Capital Formation** An entrepreneur is helpful in capital formation as we know that increase in the rate of capital formation is quite essential for the economic development of any country. Those nations which are not able to increase the rate of capital formation or does it nominally remain backward from industrial development's point of view.
- **Increase in Employment Opportunities** An entrepreneur creates maximum employment opportunities in the society by way of establishing new industries, developing and expanding the existing industries and by undertaking innovative activities.

- **Development of New Production Techniques** An entrepreneur does not feel contended only with the existing techniques of production. Hence, he carries out various experiments for saving time, labour and capital in the production, as also to improve the variety and quality of the product and service.
- **Visionary Leader** An entrepreneur has a good vision towards the achievement of his goals. He is able to recognise profitable opportunities and conceptualise strategies.
- **Contribution of the Execution of Government Policies** An entrepreneur provide an important contribution in implementing government policies and achieving the national goals. An entrepreneurs cooperate with the government for implementations of development plans of the country.
- **Higher Productivity** Entrepreneur have the ability to produce more goods and services with less inputs. They play an important role in raising productivity.
- **Initiator** An entrepreneur is the one who initiates the process of creating an enterprise by coming up with the idea for the business and planning out how to turn that idea into reality.
- **Backbone of Capitalist System** Capitalist economy is one in which there is a freedom to save and invest to compete and operate any business. An entrepreneur plays a vital and prominent role in the enterprise because he controls market by assuming the role of a competitor and a leader.
- **Ingredient of Modern Production System** An entrepreneur has become the 'balancing wheel' of modern global economy. They seek the unique product, change the technical frontiers and reshape public desires. Today, entrepreneurs act as an ingredient of modem production system as they create wealth and employment.

Myths of Entrepreneurship

Entrepreneurship is a set of activities performed by the entrepreneur. It is the process of identifying opportunities in the market place. It is the attempt to create value. Many entrepreneurs believe a set of myths about entrepreneurship and the most common are as follows

- **Starting a Business is Easy** In reality, it is a very difficult and challenging process to start a successful business. The rate of failure of new ventures is very high but small entrepreneurship are comparatively easier to start.
- **Lot of Money to Finance New Business** Successful entrepreneurs design their business with little cash also.
- **Startups cannot be Financed** Under the schemes like MUDRA, entrepreneurs can raise loans from banks.
- **Talent is more Important than Industry** This is not true as the nature of industry an entrepreneur chooses greatly effects the success and growth of the business.
- **Most Startups are Successful** Mostly in the developing countries startups fail as they could not manage to earn high profits.

Advantages of Entrepreneurship

The main advantages of adopting entrepreneurship as a career are discussed below

- **Independence** An entrepreneur is himself a boss or owner and he can take all the decisions independently.
- **Exciting** Entrepreneurship can be very exciting with many entrepreneurs considering their ventures highly enjoyable. Everyday will be filled with new opportunities to challenge your determination, skills and abilities.
- **Wealth Creation** The principal focus of entrepreneurship is wealth creation and improved livelihood by means of making available goods and services. Entrepreneurial venture generates new wealth, new and improved products, services or technology form entrepreneurs, enable new markets to be developed and new wealth to be created.
- **Flexibility** As an entrepreneur you can schedule your work hours around other commitments, including quality time you would spend with your family.
- **Status** Success in entrepreneurship beings a considerable fame and prestige within the society.
- **Ambition Fulfilment** Through entrepreneurship one can fulfil his ambitions into original products or services.

Disadvantages of Entrepreneurship

Some of the disadvantages of entrepreneurship as a career are discussed below

- **Huge Amount of Time** You have to dedicate a huge amount of time to your own business. Entrepreneurship is not easy and for it to be successful, you have to take a level of time commitment.
- **Risk** An entrepreneurship involves high risk of loss. If the business fails then it will wipe away all the personal savings.
- **Hard Work** An entrepreneur has to work very hard to make the new business very successful.
- **Uncertain Income** There is no regular or fixed income available to an entrepreneur. So, there is uncertain kind of income received by an entrepreneur.
- **Incompetent Staff** A new entrepreneur may not be able to hire qualified and experienced staff so there are chances of incompetency by the staff due to lack of experience and knowledge.

Chapter Practice

PART 1 Objective Questions

• Multiple Choice Questions

1. Innovation of an entrepreneur includes

(a) division of work

(b) opening new markets

(c) introducing new products

(d) Both (b) and (c)

Ans. (*d*) Entreprenour creates new businesses based on innovative ideas. New goods and services offered by entrepreneurial ventures stimulate growth in the related businesses, pushing up the overall growth of an economy. Thus, innovation of an entrepreneur includes opening new markets and introducing new products.

2. Which of the following is a disadvantage of entrepreneurship as a career?

(a) Uncertainty

(b) Independency

(c) Ambition fulfilment

(d) None of the above

Ans. (*a*) Entrepreneurship does not guarantee 100% success. Entrepreneurship is a risky proposition. If you have not done your calculations right, the business might fail or may not achieve the success you initially thought. Thus, one of the disadvantage of entrepreneurship as a career is uncertainty.

3. Which of the following does an entrepreneur perform to achieve his goals?

(a) Advertisement and publicity

(b) Appointment of selling agents

(c) Both (a) and (b)

(d) New organisation structure

Ans. (*c*) Entrepreneurs create new businesses that offer new goods and services and create new type of employments. New ventures can stimulate the related businesses or sectors that support them. These have a positive cascading effect on the entire economy of a country. Thus, to find a suitable market, an entrepreneur performs advertisement and publicity, appointment of selling agents.

4. In which situation an entrepreneur will not be able to convince his fellow beings? If he/she is

(a) low self-confident (b) innovative

(c) risk-taker (d) None of these

Ans. (*a*) Entrepreneurs are confident that they will make their business succeed. They exude that confidence in everthing they do. An entrepreneur will only be able to convince his fellow beings, if he/she is low self-confident.

5. Incompetent staff means

(a) experienced staff

(b) qualified staff

(c) not experienced and qualified staff

(d) None of the above

Ans. (*c*) Entrepreneurs should hire competent staff who are well-qualified and experienced according to the nature of the work to be done. Incompetent staff should not be hired because they are not experienced and qualified staff.

6. How does an entrepreneur can get the work done from his/her team?

(a) By creating a spirit of teamwork

(b) By motivation

(c) Both (a) and (b)

(d) Using harsh words and actions

Ans. (*c*) An entrepreneur should be able to motivate his/her team to perform their best. He/She is responsible for the ill/high spirit of a team by motivating them positively. An entrepreneur can get the work done from his/her team by motivating them.

7. Which of the following is/are the function(s) of an entrepreneur?

(a) Innovation (b) Risk taking

(c) Decision-making (d) All of these

Ans. (*d*) An entrepreneur should be innovative who can introduce new products, raw materials and organisation structure. An entrepreneur should be able to take choose one among various alternatives, the end results of which are unpredictable. An entrepreneur should be able to take decision on their own.

8. Which of the following is an advantage of entrepreneurship as a career?

(a) Risk (b) Hardwork

(c) Independence (d) None of these

Ans. (*c*) An entrepreneur is his own boss. He can take all decisions himself. He need not obey someone. Thus, an advantage of entrepreneurship as a career is his/her independence in the field of work.

9. Decision-making function of entrepreneur includes
(a) Hardwork
(b) Risk bearing
(c) Utilisation of financial resources
(d) Innovative

Ans. (*b*) Decision-making function of an entrepreneur is subjected to risk as there is always uncertainty around whether the decision will lead to good or bad for the future.

10. 'An entrepreneur has to get the work done through others.' Which characteristic of the entrepreneur does this statement depict?
(a) Motivator (b) Organiser
(c) Innovator (d) None of these

Ans. (*a*) An entrepreneur motivates his/her team members to work hard and get the work done by them timely and positively.

11. Which of the following characteristics should an entrepreneur have?
(a) Innovativeness (b) Motivator
(c) Goal-oriented (d) All of these

Ans. (*d*) An entrepreneur incorporates his/her innovative ideas to work. He/She is also a motivator as they inspires/motivates his/her teammates to get their work done. He/She must be goal-oriented as without a fixed goal the work cannot be done.

12. Rehnuma has two people who work for her. Every day, she spends one hour with them to learn about what they have done that day. This means she
(a) Creates a new product
(b) Divides income
(c) Manages the business
(d) Innovates a product

Ans. (*c*) She manages the business by listening of the work done by them, learning about their problems and motivating them for future work to be done.

13. Which of the following statement is true about entrepreneurship?
(a) A lot of money is needed to start an entrepreneurial venture.
(b) Entrepreneurial ventures are mostly successful.
(c) Entrepreneurial ventures are easy to start.
(d) Most of the entrepreneurial ventures end up as failures.

Ans. (*a*) Raising the necessary funds is very difficult for an entrepreneur. A business can be started with limited money. *For example*, Infosys Technology was started with only ₹10,000. In the beginning you can hire space and equipment.Thus, a lot of money is required to start an entrepreneurial venture.

14. Which of these is the main aim of entrepreneurship?
(a) Earning profit
(b) Providing innovative products and services
(c) Both (a) and (b)
(d) Neither (a) nor (b)

Ans. (*c*) An entrepreneur earns profit by providing new and innovative products and services to the people. An entrepreneur does not believe in luck or fate. He believes in his own firm decisions and actions. He has trust in his perseverance and creations. He pulls his own strings. Thus, the main aim of entrepreneurship is earning profit and providing innovative products and services.

15. Mary buys bulbs for her business from Noida. She learns that bulbs are cheaper in Faridabad. So, she decides to start buying bulbs from there.
(a) Make decisions
(b) Divide income
(c) Take risks
(d) Goal-oriented

Ans. (*a*) Mary takes the decision on her own which is best for her business.

• Case Based MCQs

Direction *Read the case and answer the following questions.*

16. Entrepreneurship development is the process of improving the skills and knowledge of entrepreneurs through various training and classroom programs. Entrepreneurship development is concerned with the study of entrepreneurial behaviour, the dynamics of business set-up, development and expansion of the enterprise. The whole point of entrepreneurship development is to increase the number of entrepreneurs. This accelerates employment generation and economic development.
Entrepreneurship is promoted to help lessen the unemployment problem, to overcome the problem of stagnation and to increase the competitiveness and growth of business and industries.
Entrepreneurship development concentrates more on growth potential and innovation.
Entrepreneurship development has gained increasing significance in developing an economy. It is an organised and systematic development. It is a tool of industrialisation and a solution to unemployment problem for any country.

(i) Which of the following is the concern related to the study of entrepreneurship development?
(a) Entrepreneurial behaviour
(b) Dynamics of business set-up
(c) Development and expansion of the enterprise
(d) All of the above

(ii) Which of the following is a tool of industrialisation and a solution to unemployment problem for any country?
(a) Entrepreneur
(b) Entrepreneurship
(c) Entrepreneurship development
(d) None of the above

(iii) The whole point of entrepreneurship development is related to
(a) increase the number of stakeholders
(b) increase the number of entrepreneurs
(c) decrease the number of shoppers
(d) increase the number of developers

(iv) Which of the following does entrepreneurship development does not accelerate?
(a) Employment generation (b) Economic development
(c) Stagnation of resources (d) All of these

(v) Which of the following statement(s) is/are true about entrepreneurship development?
(a) Entrepreneurship development is an organised and systematic development.
(b) Entrepreneurship development concentrates more on growth potential and innovation.
(c) Entrepreneurship development is the process of improving the skills and knowledge of entrepreneurs through various training and classroom programs.
(d) All of the above

Ans. (i) (*d*) Entrepreneurship development is a study of the dynamics of being an entrepreneur. It depicts the exact behaviour of an entrepreneur that he/she should follow for the development and expansion of the enterprise.

(ii) (*c*) Entrepreneurship development is a solution of unemployment for the youth of the society and leads a country towards its development and upliftment.

(iii) (*b*)Entrepreneurship development is to inspire the youth for being an entrepreneur and thus to increase the number of entrepreneurs of a country.

(iv) (*c*) Entrepreneurship development accelerates the solution to the problem of stagnation of resources as their will always be a flow of resources without any logging.

(v) (*d*) Entrepreneurship development concentrates on economic and potential growth of a country as it promotes innovativeness, decision-making, risk-bearer and many more. Entrepreneurs have the ability to produce more goods and services with less inputs. They play an important role in raising productivity.

17. Business includes all those economic activities which are concerned with the production/purchase and sale or exchange of goods and services with the objective of earning profits. A business enterprise is an economic institution as it is engaged in the production and/or distribution of products and services in order to earn profits. A factory owner, a shopkeeper, a transport company, an insurance company, a commercial bank, an advertising agency, etc., are examples of business enterprises. Hence, business may be defined as an economic activity involving the production and sale of goods and services to earn profits by satisfying human needs.

On the other hand, entrepreneurship is the process of discovering an opportunity, mobilising resources, launching an enterprise to explore the opportunity. It is an attempt to create value. Business and entrepreneurship are complementary to each other and cannot be separated.

(i) What is the name given to the process of discovering an opportunity, mobilising resources, launching an enterprise to exploit the opportunity?
(a) Entrepreneurship
(b) Entrepreneurship development
(c) Entrepreneurship activities
(d) Entrepreneur

(ii) In which of the following activity a business enterprise is involved?
(a) Production and/or distribution of products and services in order to earn profits.
(b) Discovering an opportunity and mobilising resources.
(c) Launching an enterprise to exploit the opportunity.
(d) All of the above

(iii) Which of the following is/are complementary to each other?
(a) Entrepreneurship and marketing
(b) Business and sales
(c) Business and entrepreneurship
(d) Business and marketing

(iv) Which of the following is/are example(s) of business activities?
(a) An advertising company
(b) A factory owner
(c) A transport owner
(d) All of the above

(v) Which of the following statement(s) is/are false about business?

(a) Business may be defined as an economic activity involving the production.
(b) Business is concerned about the sale of goods and services to earn profits by satisfying human needs.
(c) Both (a) and (b)
(d) Business is an attempt to create value.

Ans. (i) (*a*) According to the National Knowledge Commission (NKC), "Entrepreneurship is the set of activities performed by an entrepreneur." Thus, entrepreneur precedes entrepreneurship.

An entrepreneurship deals with discovering an opportunity, utilising and mobilising resources, launching an enterprise to explore the opportunity.

(ii) (*a*) A business enterprise is much different from an entrepreneurship. A business enterprise mainly subjected to economic activities profit/loss and many more. Whereas an entrepreneurship is basically concerned about the overall development of their company with their country.

(iii) (*c*) Business and entrepreneurship are complementary to each other as they are different in the way they both operate. Business is about profit/loss statement and entrepreneurship is about growth.

(iv) (*d*) The business activities given in the options are not innovative in any essence of work. These are traditional business that are going round. Thus, these (an advertising company, a factory owner, a transport owner) are business activities.

(v) (*d*) Business is not an attempt to create value whereas an entrepreneurship business is all about traditional work which does not involve innovativeness. Entrepreneurship is concerned with creating new products, innovative ideas and to create value of the products.

PART 2
Subjective Questions

• Short Answer Type Questions

1. What is the contribution of the entrepreneurs in the execution of government policies?

Ans. The entrepreneurs provide an important contribution in implementing government policies and achieving the national goals. They cooperate with the government for implementations of development plans of the country.

2. What is entrepreneurship development?

Ans. Entrepreneurship development is the process of improving the knowledge and skills of the entrepreneurs. In other words, it can be said that entrepreneurship development is the process of enhancing an entrepreneur's ability to develop, manage and organise a business venture, while keeping in mind the risks associated with it.

3. What do you mean by the term entrepreneurial skills?

Ans. Entrepreneurial skills are the basic skills that help an entrepreneur to start, develop, finance and successfully run a business. Every entrepreneur who is starting a business must have a complete knowledge of the various aspects of his/her business, not only for the success of his venture; but also for its growth and expansion.

4. Explain the risk bearing characteristic of an entrepreneur.

Ans. An entrepreneur has to have patience to see his efforts bearfruit. In the intervening period (time gap between the conception and implementation of an idea and its results), an entrepreneur has to assume risk. If an entrepreneur does not have the willingness to assume risk, entrepreneurship would never succeed.

5. Explain the role of an entrepreneur as a catalytic agent.

Ans. As Joseph Schumpeter says, entrepreneur's task is "creative destruction". He destroys to create new things. He changes and transmutes values. He searches change and responds to it. He is a change creator. Ralph Harwitz writes in his book 'Realities of Profitability', The entrepreneur makes a happening, wants piece of action, is the growth man. Without him there is no happening, no action, no growth.

6. Explain the quality of an entrepreneur as a passionate person.

Ans. Successful entrepreneurs are passionate about making their business succeed. They genuinely love their work and are willing to put in extra hours to make their business succeed. Success gives them a joy that goes beyond money.

7. State a difference between an entrepreneur and a businessman.

Ans. An entrepreneur is different from a conventional businessman. A businessman is someone who sets up a business with an existing idea offering products and services to customers. An entrepreneur, on the other hand, is a person who starts an enterprise with a new idea or concept or a better way to offer an existing idea or concept.

8. What is a business plan?

Ans. An entrepreneur conducts studies to assess the feasibility of the market as regards the proposed products or services. He makes an assessment of the resources required to run the enterprise and the problems that may possibly be faced. Such a blue print of an enterprise is termed as a business plan or a project report.

9. Why an entrepreneur is considered as an 'enterprising man'?

Ans. A business does not get started by itself. It is the entrepreneur who takes the risks and is willing to face devastating failure. He braves uncertainty, strikes out on his own wit, devotion to duty and singleness of purpose, somehow creates business and industrial activity where none existed before. His values and activities have become integral to corporate culture.

10. How does an entrepreneur promotes economic prosperity of a country?

Ans. Entrepreneurs can bring about drastic changes in the very structure of the economy. They stand beyond challenges and make huge profits in every economic system. They are an important source of economic development. They create jobs, wealth and capital in the country. They promote investment, increase production and bring competitiveness in business, reduce costs of products and raise the standard of living in society.

11. Why an entrepreneur is highly optimistic?

Ans. A successful entrepreneur is always optimistic and is not disturbed by the present problems faced by him. He is always optimistic that the situation will become favourable for business in future.

12. Explain the role and significance of entrepreneurs.

Ans. The role and significance of entrepreneurs are discussed below

(i) **Organiser of Society's Productive Resources** An entrepreneur is the organises of society's productive resources. He is the person who assembles the unused natural, physical and human resources of the society, combines them properly, establishes effective coordination between them and makes the economic activities dynamic.

(ii) **Helpful in Capital Formation** An entrepreneur is helpful in capital formation or we know that increase in the rate of capital formation is quite essential for the economic development of any country.

(iii) **Increase in Employment Opportunities** An entrepreneur creates maximum employment opportunities in the society by way of establishing new industries, developing and expanding the existing industries and by undertaking innovative activities.

13. What are the myths of entrepreneurship? Explain.

Ans. The myths of entrepreneurship are as follows

(i) **It is Easy to Start a Business** This depends on the scale of the enterprise. Starting up a large entrepreneurial venture is a challenging process. Small scale enterprises are easier to set up. Moreover, the rate of failure of new ventures is quite high all over the world. Just about one-third of all enterprises become profitable only after operating for several years.

(ii) **Lot of Money is needed to Startup a New Venture** Again, this depends on the type and scale of the business venture. There are ventures that can be started with a small amount of money. Big ventures need a lot of investment.

(iii) **A Startup cannot Borrow from the Banks** Today our government is promoting startup ventures and offering them loans on easy terms under various government schemes such as MUDRA (Micro-units Development and Refinance Agency) and MSME (Micro, Small & Medium Enterprises) scheme.

(iv) **Businesses either Flourish or Fail** This is not always the case. Some ventures initially falter or have lackluster growth rates. However, with right re-planning and effort they may go on to achieve a healthy growth.

(v) **A Good Idea is the only Requirement for a Successful Enterprise** Remember that even the best of ideas need proper execution to become a reality. Ideas are important, but so are planning, talent, leadership, communication and a host of other factors.

14. Define an entrepreneur. Explain the leadership and decision-making qualities of an entrepreneur.

Ans. An entrepreneur is someone who perceives opportunity, organises resources needed for exploiting that opportunity and exploits it.

An entrepreneurial leader realises the importance of initiative and reactiveness as they go out of their way to provide all support to the team.

Decision-making is an important function because it includes stabilising organisation's aims and objectives and changes them according to the changing conditions.

15. Explain the role and significance of an entrepreneur as an enterprising man and a visionary leader.

Ans. **Enterprising Man** A business does not get started by itself. It is the entrepreneur who takes the risks and is willing to face devastating failure. He braves uncertainty, strikes out on his own and through native wit, devotion to duty and singleness of purpose, somehow creates business and industrial activity where none existed before. His values and activities have become integral to corporate culture.

Visionary Leader An entrepreneur has a good vision and sense of mission. He instills inspiration.

He is able to recognise potentially profitable opportunities and to conceptualise the venture strategy. He is the key force in successfully moving the idea from the laboratory to the market place. He has the sense of accomplishment.

16. Do you think an entrepreneur is innovative by nature? Discuss.

Ans. Customer's requirements and tastes keep on changing, therefore, production should meet the customer's requirements. Thus, innovativeness is another important characteristic of an entrepreneur. He always tries to out strive others by taking initiative in doing new things, i.e. exploring new products, new markets, new raw materials, new methods of production etc.

17. Do you think entrepreneur is a leader? Discuss.

Ans. An entrepreneur is essentially a leader. According to K.L. Sharma, a psychologist, entrepreneurs are men who exhibit qualities of leadership in solving problems. They have to lead a team for achievement of goals. Thus, an entrepreneur must have all universally accepted qualities of a leader, i.e. initiative, high energy level, self-confidence, human relations skills, motivational skills, creativity and keen desire to solve problems.

18. Explain the creative and determined nature of an entrepreneur.

Ans. **Creativity** Creativity is probably the most important trait of an entrepreneur. Entrepreneurs often come up with innovative solutions and repurpose their products to market them to new industries. Repurposing means transforming a product for an alternative use.

Determination Successful entrepreneurs do not believe that something cannot be done. They make determined efforts and work hard to achieve success in all their endeavours.

• Long Answer Type Questions

19. Explain characteristics or qualities of an entrepreneur.

Ans. The characteristics of successful entrepreneurs are as follows

(i) **Goal-oriented** Entrepreneur is goal-oriented. Firstly, he sets a goal to achieve, i.e. to earn profit by producing goods and services and after reaching one goal he proceeds to another goal.

(ii) **Highly Optimistic** A successful entrepreneur is always optimistic and is not disturbed by the present problems faced by him. He is always optimistic that the situation will become favourable for business in future.

(iii) **Trust in Self** An entrepreneur does not believe in luck or fate. He believes in his own firm decisions and actions. He has trust in his perseverance and creations. He pulls his own strings.

(iv) **Leadership** An entrepreneur must possess the characteristics of leadership and must lead a ream for achievement of goals. The leader is able to clearly articulate their ideas and has a clear vision.

(v) **Innovativeness** With the changing needs and requirements of customers production should meet requirements with the help in innovative ideas.

An entrepreneur does not have to restrict itself to just one innovation rather he must use combination of innovation.

(vi) **Decision-maker** An entrepreneur has to take many decisions to put his business idea into reality. He chooses the best suitable and profitable alternative.

20. What are the functions of an entrepreneur? Explain.

Ans. The functions of an entrepreneur are as follows

(i) **New Inventions** Encouraging new inventions and introducing innovations in production, production techniques, sales, marketing, advertisement etc.

(ii) **Establishing Relations with Government** To establish relations with government and its functionaries. In this regards his functions are (a) obtaining licences, (b) payment of taxes, (c) selling the product to government, (d) Provision for export-import etc.

(iii) **Size and Scale of Business Unit** To decide about size of business unit, i.e., he wants to establish one production unit or more etc. which is dependent upon demand of the product. Similarly, he has to decide about scale of production, i.e., small scale, middle scale or large scale.

(iv) **Organisation and Management** An entrepreneur organises and manages various economic and human factors through planning, coordination, control, supervision and direction.

(v) **Factors of Production** Another important function of an entrepreneur is the factors of production i.e. land, labour, capital etc., should be in right proportion and to maximise output of these factors is the responsibility of the entrepreneur.

21. Explain the role of an entrepreneur as "Person with higher productivity" and "Ingredient of modern production system."

Ans. **Person with Higher Productivity** Entrepreneurs have the ability to produce more goods and services with less inputs. They play an important role in raising productivity. *John Kendrick Bangs* writes, "Higher productivity is chiefly a matter of improving production techniques, and this task is the entrepreneurial function par excellence." Two keys to higher productivity are research and development and investment in new plant and machinery. But there is a close link between R & D and investment programmes, with a higher entrepreneurial input into both.

Ingredient of Modern Production System Entrepreneur has become the 'balancing wheel' of modern global economy. They seek the unique product, the marketing breakthrough. They change technical frontiers and reshape public desires. They create wealth and employment.

22. Discuss the importance of entrepreneurship.

Ans. If we go through the business history of India, we come across many names who have emerged as successful entrepreneurs, like Tatas, Birlas, Dalmia, Modi, Ambani etc. These business houses started as small scale enterprises and have made their name in the list of industrialists of world fame.

The success of small enterprises and their growth to leading industrial houses can be attributed to entrepreneurs themselves. Thus, it is important to understand the success story of such entrepreneurs. There are definitely some common personal characteristics in entrepreneurs.

The entrepreneur is in essence an institution which comprises of all people required to perform various functions. The task of such people is to innovate, adjust or combine various factors of production, and expand on account of change in demand and market conditions. They must acknowledge the opportunities and must also be in a position to make opportunities out of a given situation.

(i) **It give Freedom** An entrepreneur is himself a boss or owner and he can take all the decisions independently.

(ii) **It can be Exciting** Entrepreneurship can be very exciting with many entrepreneurs considering their ventures highly enjoyable. Every day will be filled with new opportunities to challenge your determination, skills and abilities.

(iii) **It Allows to Set your own Earnings** The principal focus of entrepreneurship is wealth creation and improved livelihood by means of making available goods and services. Entrepreneurial ventures generate new wealth. New and improved products, services or technology from entrepreneurs, enable new markets to be developed and new wealth to be created.

(iv) **If offers Flexibility** As an entrepreneur you can schedule your work hours around other commitments, including quality time you would spend with your family.

(v) **Status** Success in entrepreneurship brings a considerable fame and prestige within the society.

(vi) **It offers Ambition-fulfilment** Through entrepreneurship one can fulfil his ambitions into original products or services.

23. Describe the disadvantages of entrepreneurship as a career.

Ans. Some of the common disadvantages of entrepreneurship as a career are as follows

(i) **Huge Amount of Time** You have to dedicate a huge amount of time to your own business. Entrepreneurship is not easy and for it to be successful, you have to take a level of time commitment.

(ii) **Risk** Entrepreneurship involves high risk of loss. If the business fails then it will wipe away all the personal savings.

(iii) **Hard Work** Entrepreneur has to work very hard to make the new business very successful.

(iv) **Uncertain Amount** There is no regular or fixed income available to an entrepreneur. So, there is always uncertainty in terms of income.

(v) **Incompetent Staff** A new entrepreneur may not be able to hire qualified and experienced staff so there are chances of incompetency by the staff due to lack of experience and knowledge.

Chapter Test

Multiple Choice Questions

1. Which of these is not a characteristic of a successful entrepreneur?
(a) Risk taking (b) Determination
(c) Nature lover (d) Innovativeness

2. An entrepreneur is the .... of society's productive resources.
(a) organiser (b) developer
(c) innovator (d) producer

3. An entrepreneur has to take .... by choosing one among various alternatives.
(a) risk (b) coordination
(c) action (d) trust

4. An entrepreneur has a good .... and sense of ....
(a) vision, mission (b) mission, losing
(c) vision, motivation (d) motivation, betrayal

5. Ravi's customer comes to his store and starts shouting at him. He does not get angry. He listens to what his customer is saying. He is ....
(a) hardworking (b) confident
(c) patient (d) prying new ideas

6. Susheela decides to sell her company tyres in Sri Lanka. It does not sell and she has a loss. She apologises to the people who work for her. She says she will plan better next time. She ....
(a) takes responsibility for your mistakes
(b) thinks before making a decision
(c) does not give up
(d) is creative

Short Answer Type Questions

7. Define the term entrepreneurship.

8. Write any two characteristics of a successful entrepreneur.

9. Discuss the role of an entrepreneur as a great achiever.

10. Explain the role of an entrepreneur as a protector of society's interests?

Long Answer Type Questions

11. Explain the function of an entrepreneur as a decision-maker.

12. Discuss the relationship between entrepreneurship and society.

13. Explain how entrepreneurs are considered as "first movers" and "Person who creates job".

Answers

Multiple Choice Questions

1. (c) *2. (a)* *3. (a)* *4. (a)* *5. (c)* *6. (c)*

For Detailed Solutions
Scan the code

CHAPTER 02

Green Skills-II

In this Chapter...

- Sustainable Development
- Importance of Sustainable Development
- Problems Related to Sustainable Development
- Solutions for Sustainable Development
- Short-Term Solutions
- Long-Term Solutions

Sustainable Development

Sustainable development is a development that meets the needs of the present without compromising the ability of future generations to meet their own needs.

The important principles of sustainable development are as follows

- To carefully utilise all resources.
- To conserve resources so that they meet the demands and requirements of the future generations.
- To minimise the depletion of natural resources.
- Respect and care for all forms of life.
- People should learn to conserve the natural resources in order to protect the living beings.
- Conserving the Earth's vitality and diversity.
- Improving the quality of human life.
- Changing personal attitude and practices towards the environment.

Sustainable development is the organising principle for meeting human development goals. It has its roots in ideas about sustainable forest management which were developed in Europe during the 17th and 18th centuries. The idea of sustainable development gained wide acceptance due to environmental concerns in the 20th century. The concept of sustainable development was popularised in 1987 by the United Nations World Commission on Environment and Development. In its Our Common Future Report or Brundtland Report it defined the idea as "Development that meets the needs of the present, without compromising the ability of future generations to meet their needs."

Importance of Sustainable Development

Sustainable development is necessary for the maintenance of the environment. The importance of sustainable development are as follows

- **Proper Use of Means and Resources** Sustainable development teaches people to make use of means and resources for the maximum benefit without wastage. It helps to conserve and promote the environment.
- **Development of Positive Attitude** Sustainable development brings about changes in people's knowledge, attitude and skills. It aware the people the responsibility to use and preserve natural resources. It creates the feeling that natural resources are the common property of all and nobody can use the property according to his personal will. It helps to conserve natural and social environment.
- **Development Based on People's Participation** People's participation is to be given priority in development work in order to achieve the aim of sustainable development. It creates the interest of local people in development work and environment conservation with the feeling of ownership.

- **Limitation of Development** Limited but effective use of means and resources are enough for the people to satisfy their basic needs. Limited and non-renewable means and resources go on decreasing in globally due to over-use. Development works should be conducted as per carrying capacity.
- **Long Lasting Development** Sustainable development aims at achieving the goal of economic and social development without destroying the Earth's means and resources. It attempts to create the concept of maintaining the present work for the future and conserving the natural resources for future generation.

  So, due to the realisation of importance of sustainable development, now there is a transcending concern for survival of the people and planet. We need to take a holistic view of the very basis of our existence. It is important to reconcile ambitious economic development and preserving the natural resources and ecosystem.
- **Sustainable Development Goals** Sustainable development has three main components economy, environment and social inclusion. It seeks to ensure economic development, while protecting the environment through participation of the societies and communities. The United Nations Sustainable Development Summit 2015, has set seventeen specific goals towards achieving sustainable development. Given are summarised in the graphic below

Problems Related to Sustainable Development

Some problems related to sustainable development are as follows

- Poor management of natural resources combined with growing economic activities will continue to pose serious challenges to environment.
- The most significant environmental problems are associated with resources that are renewable such as air and water. They have finite capacity to assimilate emissions and wastes but if pollution exceeds this capacity ecosystem can deteriorate rapidly.
- To assess the regenerative capacity of natural resources is difficult. In the cases of soil erosion, atmospheric pollution etc., there is substantial uncertainty about the extent and outcomes of environmental degradation.
- The overall effects of economic activities on the environment are continuously changing.
- Due to rise in income, the demands for improvement in environmental quality will increase as well as the resources available for investment but it is not mandatory in some cases as problems are observed to get worse as income rise.
- Rise in population is another problem that would further lead to severe environmental degradation in the future.
- Another challenge is rise in demand for energy as it is estimated that the total manufacturing outputs in developing countries will increase to about six times the current levels by 2030.

Another challenge is rise in demand of food crops with the growth of population. To protect fragile soils and natural habitats, this will have to be achieved by raising yields on existing crop land.

Solutions for Sustainable Development

Inspite of difficult circumstances sustainable development is achievable however, it would require a lots of concentrated and coordinated effort. The achievement of sustainable development requires the integration of economic, environmental and social components at all levels.

Short-Term Solutions

The short-term solutions related to sustainable development are as follows

- The practice of illegal deforestation and smuggling of forest resources should be stopped.
- Proper balance ought to be maintained between deforestation and afforestation.
- Planning and building of industrial zones to manage and process are types of wastes.
- Proper treatment system, recycling of waste and their proper disposal should be undertaken.
- Adoption of Rainwater Harvesting Techniques, drip/sprinkler irrigation and use of alternative sources of energy.
- Less chemical fertilizers should be used along with environment-friendly pesticides and weedicides.
- Polluting industries should be relocated outside the cities, far away from the populated areas.

Long-Term Solutions

The long-term solutions related to sustainable development are as follows

- Government should make policies against illegal activities.
- Awareness campaigns should be launched for farmers and industrialists.

- Ecology must be protected through imposition of taxes and fines.
- Practice of sustainable agriculture must be promoted such as permaculture, agroforestry, mixed farming, multiple cropping and crop rotation.

United Nations Sustainable Development Summit (2015) sets global development goals. These goals are termed as Agenda 2030. The goals are as follows

- End poverty in all forms everywhere.
- End hunger, achieve food security and improved nutrition and promote sustainable agriculture.
- Ensure healthy lives and well-being for all.
- Ensure inclusive and quality education for all and promote lifelong learning.
- Achieve gender equality and empower all women and girls.
- Ensure access to water and sanitation for all.
- Ensure access to affordable, reliable, sustainable and modern energy for all.
- Promote inclusive and sustainable economic growth, employment and decent work for all.
- Build resilient infrastructure, promote sustainable industrialisation and foster innovation.
- Reduce inequality within and among countries.
- Make cities inclusive, safe, resilient and production.
- Ensure sustainable consumption and production.
- Take urgent action to combat climate change and its impacts.
- Conserve and sustainably use oceans, seas and marine resources.
- Sustainably manage forests, halt and reverse land degradation, halt biodiversity loss.
- Promote peaceful and inclusive societies.
- Revitalise the global partnership for sustainable development.

Chapter Practice

PART 1 Objective Questions

• Multiple Choice Questions

1. Sustainable forest management were developed in Europe during the centuries.

(a) 16th and 18th (b) 17th and 18th
(c) 18th and 19th (d) 19th and 20th

Ans. (*b*) Sustainable forest management were developed in Europe during the 17th and 18th centuries. The idea of sustainable development became widely accepted during the 20th century due to the raised environmental issues.

2. Do you agree with the view that greater economic activity will certainly lead to greater damage to the environment?

(a) Yes (b) No
(c) Not certainly (d) Cannot be said

Ans. (*a*) As for the greater economic activities trees are cut down, forest are removed to make roads, buildings, etc and thus it leads to greater damage to the environment.

3. Sustainable development is necessary because

(a) it helps to promote and conserve the environment
(b) it aware the people for effective use of natural resources
(c) it aims at achieving the goal of economic and social development
(d) All of the above

Ans. (*d*) Sustainable development is necessary/important as it promotes and conserves the environment for future necessities. It makes the people aware for the effective use of natural resources like air, water, soil, minerals and forests. It aims at achieving the goal of economic and social development of the people tend to love in the society.

4. Which of these is non-renewable source of energy?

(a) Wind power (b) Solar power
(c) Hydroelectricity (d) Coal

Ans. (*d*) A non-renewable resource is a natural resource that cannot be readily replaced by natural means at a pace quick enough to keep up with consumption. There are four major types of non-renewable resources: oil, natural gas, coal and nuclear energy.

5. The concept of sustainable development is

(a) easy and practicable
(b) too subjective and complex
(c) an utopian idea which can never be put into practice
(d) All of the above

Ans. (*b*) The concept of sustainable development is too subjective and complex as the needs of the present generation had to fulfilled by keeping in mind about the future ones. It is not an easy task to be performed and also at the same time not an utopian task.

6. If sustainable development is neglected, then

(a) we shall have a safe and secure environment
(b) it will destroy ecology and environment endangering the survival of future generation
(c) mankind will continue to live and prosper
(d) All of the above

Ans. (*b*) If sustainable development is neglected, then it will destroy both flora and fauna. The future generation will not be having non-renewable resources as it is limited in matter. Thus, endangering the survival of future generation.

7. What is the most serious problem as far as sustainable development in agriculture is concerned?

(a) To raise yields on existing croplands without extending the area under cultivation.
(b) To raise yields by extending the area under cultivation.
(c) Both (a) and (b)
(d) None of the above

Ans. (*a*) The serious problem in the field of agriculture is that to raise the quality and quantity of crops to be grown on existing cropland instead of increasing the land under cultivation.

8. Why is it important to adopt sustainable development?

(a) To save ecology and environment

(b) To save mankind

(c) Both (a) and (b)

(d) None of the above

Ans. (*c*) It is very important to adopt sustainable development for each individual on this Earth to save our environment for the existence of both flora(plants) and fauna(animals). Humans are the only living beings, who can make extensive modifications to their natural environment.

9. We need to realise our moral and ethical obligations to

(a) mother Earth

(b) to our future generations

(c) Both (a) and (b)

(d) None of the above

Ans. (*c*) We need to realise our ethical and moral obligations to the mother Earth. Human beings are caretakers of the planet and responsible trustees of the legacy of future generations.

10. Which of the following is a major problem of sustainable development?

(a) Turning the concept of sustainability into framing policies and rules.

(b) Striking a balance between development and its consequent damages to the environment.

(c) Both (a) and (b)

(d) None of the above

Ans. (*c*) Sustainable development is a form of development that aims to fulfil the needs of the present generation of humans while keeping the needs of the future generations in mind.

In order to incorporate the concept of sustainable development, some policies and rules are to be framed. The problem arises when to frame the policies and rules and also at the time of implementation. A major problem is also to strike a balance in nature due to the economic development of the society.

11. .... jobs that contribute substantially to preserving or restoring the natural environment.

(a) Green (b) Green-collared

(c) Either (a) or (b) (d) None of these

Ans. (*c*) Green or green-collared jobs are jobs that contribute substantially to preserving or restoring the natural environment. This includes jobs that help to protect ecosystems and biodiversity.

12. What is the green economy?

(a) A green economy is one that promotes economic development while making sure that the environment is protected.

(b) A green economy is one that promotes social development of the country.

(c) A green economy is one that promotes education among children.

(d) None of the above

Ans. (*a*) A green economy is one that promotes economic development while making sure that the environment is protected. In a green economy, growth in employment and income are driven by public and private investment in such economic activities, infrastructure and assets that are environmentally-friendly.

13. Achievement of sustainable development requires the integration of which component at all levels?

(a) Ecological (b) Economic and social

(c) All of these (d) None of these

Ans. (*c*) In order to achieve sustainable development, requires the integration of ecological, economic and social components. Our environment is an integral part of our existence. Without our environment our existence, itself, would not be possible.

14. United Nations Sustainable Development Summit (2015) set up development goals called as

(a) Agenda 2010 (b) Agenda 2030

(c) Agenda 2050 (d) Agenda 2040

Ans. (*b*) United Nations Sustainable Development Summit (2015) set up development goals called as Agenda 2030. By 2030, UN Sustainable Development Goals should be achieved. Sustainable development is defined as a type of development that meets the needs of the present without compromising the ability of the future generations to meet their own needs.

• Case Based MCQs

Direction *Read the case and answer the following questions.*

15. The United Nations Sustainable Development Summit, has set seventeen specific goals towards achieving sustainable development. The goals of the sustainable development give us a fair idea about the main problems and challenges that are halting the growth of sustainable practices around the world. As sustainable development tries to manage factors in three broad areas: economy, social and the environment, the problems can also be viewed from these broad areas. The problems to sustainable development can be identified as: poverty, hunger and exclusion (economic problems); unemployment, lack of social justice, war and conflicts, building peaceful and inclusive societies, building strong institutions of governance and supporting the rule of law (social problems) and environmental pollution, degradation of natural resources, loss of biodiversity global warming and climatic changes (environmental problems).

(i) What is/are the area(s) which are to be managed in order to get sustainable development?
(a) Social, economic and environmental
(b) Agriculture, economic and environmental
(c) Social, economic and user-friendly
(d) Social, drastic and environmental

(ii) Unemployment is which type of factor?
(a) Social factor (b) Economic factor
(c) Environmental factor (d) Physical factor

(iii) What is/are the problem(s) that can termed as environmental problem?
(a) Hunger (b) Pollution
(c) War and conflicts (d) All of these

(iv) What is the main aim of sustainable development?
(a) To save the resources
(b) To conserve the environment
(c) To think about the future generation
(d) All of the above

(v) United Nations Sustainable Development Summit happened in the year ....
(a) 2014 (b) 2015
(c) 2016 (d) 2020

Ans. (i) (*a*) The three broad areas which are to managed in order to achieve sustainable development are social, economic and environmental.

(ii) (*a*) Unemployment is a social factor related to achieve sustainable development. Sustainable development promotes green jobs which helps in preserving or restoring the natural environment.

(iii) (*b*) Pollution is an environmental problem and it a major problem related to achieve sustainable development. Pollution is caused by human activities resulting in pollution water, air and land.

(iv) (*d*) The main aim of sustainable development is to 'live today and think for the future.'One should try to save the resources for the future generation by limiting their consumption today.

(v) (*b*) The United Nations Sustainable Development Summit was organised in the year 2015 in which 17 sustainable goals were decided which was about to be achieved by 2030.

16. Humans are the only living beings, who can make extensive modifications to their natural environment. In this way, they are able to create an artificial environment for themselves to carry out various social, political and business activities for their development. Man has been modifying his natural environment from time immemorial and exploiting various natural resources such as soil, water, forests, wildlife, minerals etc., to fulfil his various needs. After the industrial revolution in the 18th century, the exploitation of natural resources gained unprecedented momentum. The developmental activities in the last few centuries have led to a widespread destruction of the natural environment and resulted in many environmental problems.

(i) Who can make extensive use of environment?
(a) Human (b) Animals (c) Plants (d) Resources

(ii) Which of the following is/are natural resource(s)?
(a) Petrol (b) Coal
(c) Soil (d) Diesel

(iii) After which activity, the natural resources are exploited unprecedently?
(a) Pollution
(b) Industrial revolution
(c) Due to the outcome of Brundtland Report
(d) None of the above

(iv) Which of these is/are an integral part of the existence of human being?
(a) Environment (b) Wealth
(c) Luxuries (d) All of these

(v) Which of the following human activities impacted the nature?
(a) We remove water from rivers, lakes and aquifers for drinking and cleaning.
(b) We fulfil our food-related needs from both wild and fanned plants and animals.
(c) We cut down trees to get timber that is used as building material.
(d) All of the above

Ans. (i) (*a*) Human can make extensive use of resources present in the environment by using their various activities. Animals do not cook food, wear clothes, require houses and may more. We require all these to live a healthy life and thus exploiting the environment.

(ii) (*c*) Soil is available naturally on Earth, thus it is natural resource. It is also abundantly available. Soil is formed when large rocks breaks down into sand and silt. We are using soil abundantly to fulfil our needs.

(iii) (*b*) Due to the evolution of industries, human started polluting and exploiting the natural resources like water, air, soil, and thus affecting the normal habitat of animals. For our own needs, trees are being cut down, resulting in the decreasing number of forests which is the natural habitat of animals. The needs of humans are exploiting the environment manifoldly.

(iv) (*a*) We have been using the resources since out the first walk on Earth. We have being using the resources abundantly and not giving anything to the nature. We can live without wealth and luxuries but not without environment. Thus, environment is an integral part of the existence of human being.

(v) (*d*) Humans have being exploiting the nature manifoldly by various activities. This shows how selfish a human can be as we are taking everything from the nature without giving it anything. We should conserve our environment for future generation by limiting our consumption of resources both renewable and non-renewable.

PART 2
Subjective Questions

• Short Answer Type Questions

1. Give the definition of sustainable development as suggested by Brundtland Report.

Ans. According to Brundtland report, development that meets the needs of the present, without compromising the ability of future generation to meet their needs is sustainable development.

2. How does sustainable development helps to manage climate change?

Ans. Climate change can be mitigated through sustainable development practices. These practices seek to reduce the use of fossil-based sources of fuel such as petrol, diesel, natural gas and coal. Fossil fuels as sources of energy are unsustainable since they will be depleted at some time. Their burning is also responsible for the emission of greenhouse gases and consequent global warming and climate change.

3. Write any three challenges to sustainable development.

Ans. Three challenges to sustainable development are

(i) Rise in population level would lead to severe environmental degradation in the future.

(ii) Poor management of natural resources combined with growing economic activities will continue to pose serious challenges to environment.

(iii) Due to rise in income, the demands for improvement in environmental quality will increase as well as the resources available for investment but it is not mandatory in some cases as problems are observed to get worse as income rise.

4. Which type of industries should be relocated outside the cities?

Ans. Polluting industries should be relocated outside the cities far away from the populated area. These industries pollute both the water and air by disposing the waste in them. The polluted is then used by animals for drinking and human beings for various activities, this leads to depletion of their health. In humans, various health issues are raised in the course of time.

5. Which serious question was raised by the first Brundt Commission Report?

Ans. One of the earliest international commissions dealing with the question of ecology and environment was the Brundt Commission. The First Brundt Report raised a very serious question, - "Are we to leave our successors a scorched planet of advancing deserts, impoverished landscapes and ailing environment?"

6. The most significant environment problems are related to which type of resources?

Ans. The most significant environmental problems are associated with resources that are renewable such as air and water. They have a finite capacity to assimilate emissions and wastes but if pollution exceeds this capacity ecosystem will deteriorate rapidly at a huge pace.

7. "Uncertainty is an inherent part of environmental problems and this uncertainty breeds complacency." Do you agree with the statement? Explain.

Ans. Yes, I agree with this statement.

Assessment of whether the regenerative capacity of a natural resource has been exceeded is difficult and complex. In the cases of soil erosion, atmospheric pollution, and loss of biodiversity, there is substantial scientific uncertainty about the extent of environmental degradation and consequences of degradation.

8. Discuss the role of sustainable development to provide financial stability.

Ans. Sustainable development practices have the ability to create more financially sustainable economies across the globe. Developing countries that cannot access fossil fuels can leverage renewable forms of energy to power their economies. From the development of renewable energy technologies, these countries can create sustainable jobs as opposed to finite jobs based on fossil fuel technologies.

9. What are the forms of sustainable agriculture?

Ans. In sustainable agriculture the production of crops takes place with the efficient use of resources without damaging the environment. Crop rotation, organic farming, use of bio-fertilizers and bio-pesticides, combining animal farming with crop farming are some examples of sustainable agricultural practices.

10. The achievement of sustainable development requires what?

Ans. The achievement of sustainable development requires the integration of economic, environmental and social components at all levels.

11. Write four development goals given by United Nations Sustainable Development Summit 2015.

Ans. Any four development goals given by United Nations Sustainable Development Summit 2015 are as follows

(i) Ensure access to affordable, reliable, sustainable and modern energy for all.

(ii) Promote inclusive and sustainable economic growth, employment and decent work for all.

(iii) Build resilient infrastructure, promote sustainable industrialisation and foster innovation.

(iv) Reduce inequality within and among countries.

12. How one can save forest from being cut?

Ans. Save and recycle paper to protect trees from being cut.

Do not buy products obtained from wild animals such as leather, fur and ivory. Collect honey without completely removing the beehives.

13. What should be done to make efficient use of electricity?

Ans. To make efficient use of electricity are as follows

(i) Don't waste electricity. Turn off lights and unplug appliances when not in use.

(ii) Select clean, renewable energy sources like solar lights.

(iii) Avoid cars or do car-pools and use cycles or public transport.

14. How one can save fisheries industry from being extinct?

Ans. In order to save fisheries industry from being extinct, one can follow a number of steps as given below

(i) Creating awareness about the harmful consequences of over-fishing.

(ii) Educating people about the sustainable fishing practices that control fishing and provide enough time for fish to breed and multiply.

(iii) Never buy endangered fish. Buy only those fish that are plentifully available and also in-season (not during the breeding season).

15. State the points through which one can manage waste.

Ans. Some points which one can manage waste are as follows

(i) Reduce, reuse and recycle before throwing away things as waste.

(ii) Use environmentally-friendly methods of waste disposal.

(iii) Use appropriate methods for recycling or disposal of the electronic and hazardous waste.

16. Why there is a need for sustainable development? Give reasons.

Ans. Sustainable development is necessary for the maintenance of the environment.

There is a need of sustainable development because of the following reasons

(i) Sustainable development teaches people to make use of means and resources for the maximum benefit without wastage.

(ii) Sustainable development brings about changes in people's knowledge, attitude and skill.

(iii) Sustainable development aims at achieving the goal of economic and social development without destroying the Earth's means and resources.

17. What will happen, if we ignore the vital signs of an ailing environment?

Ans. The Earth's vital signs reveal a patient in declining health. We need to realise our ethical and moral obligations to the mother Earth. Human beings are caretakers of the planet and responsible trustees of the legacy of future generations.

Due to the realisation of importance of sustainable development, now there is a transcending concern for survival of the people and planet. We need to take a holistic view of the very basis of our existence. The environmental problem does not necessarily signal our demise, rather it is our passport for the future.

18. Explain the short-term solutions related to sustainable development.

Ans. The short-term solutions related to sustainable development are as follows

(i) The practice of illegal deforestation and smuggling of forest resources should be stopped.

(ii) Proper balance ought to be maintained between deforestation and afforestation.

(iii) Planning and building of industrial zones to manage and process are types of wastes.

(iv) Proper treatment system, recycling of waste and their proper disposal should be undertaken.

(v) Adoption of rainwater harvesting techniques, drip/sprinkler irrigation and use of alternative sources of energy.

(vi) Less chemical fertilizers should be used along with environment-friendly pesticides and weedicides.

19. How one can take care of the environment while travelling?

Ans. In order to take care of the environment while travelling, one should follow the given points

(i) While travelling, travel in groups, limit water and energy use and avoid wastage.

(ii) Practice eco-tourism (tourism that protects the environment) and make people aware of the need of practicing eco-tourism.

(iii) Never litter around. Never damage or deface historical monuments.

(iv) Walk or cycle while going to nearby places.

(v) Use electric (battery-operated) vehicles if possible.

20. How did the idea of sustainable development originate?

Ans. The concept of sustainable forest management was developed in Europe during the 17th and 18th centuries. The idea of sustainable development gained wide acceptance due to environmental concerns in the 20th century.

The concept of sustainable development was popularised in 1987 by the "United Nations World Commission on Environment and Development." In Brundtland Report named as 'Our Common Future', defines sustainable development as "development that meets the needs of the present, without compromising the ability of future generations to meet their needs", i.e without stripping the natural world of resources future generations would need. This definition of sustainable development, which is most widely accepted now, contains two key concepts

(i) The concept of needs, in particular, the essential needs of the world's poor which should be given top most priority.

(ii) The concept of limitations imposed by the state of technology and social organisation on the environment's ability to meet present and future needs.

21. 'The concept of sustainable development is subject to criticism.' Discuss.

Ans. Criticism is the final thing that appears on introducing a new concept, as wide acceptance is almost rare.

Turning the concept of sustainability into policy raises questions about how to assess the well-being of present and future generations. The issue is more complicated because our children do not just inherit environmental pollution and resource depletion, but also enjoy the fruits of our labour, in the forms of education, skills and knowledge (i.e. human capital), as well as physical capital. They may also benefit from investments in natural resources, improvement in soil fertility and reforestation.

Thus, in considering and calculating what we pass on to future generations, we must take account of the full range of physical, human and natural capital.

22. 'Total world consumption of cereals will almost double by 2030.' Suggest measures to maintain 'sustainable development' in the light of this development.

Ans. Total world consumption of cereals will have to almost double by 2030. To protect fragile soils and natural habitats, almost all of this increase will have to be achieved by raising yields on existing cropland rather than by extending the area under cultivation. At present we are losing the forests at a fast pace. Thus, problems and challenges are formidable.

23. State the points through one can do water and forest management.

Ans. In order to do water management, one should follow the given points

(i) Use water wisely. Turn off the tap when you are not using it.

(ii) Get leaking taps and pipes fixed immediately.

(iii) Treat drain water properly before allowing it to flow into local water bodies.

In order to do forest management, one should follow the given points

(i) Save and recycle paper to protect trees from being cut.

(ii) Do not buy products obtained from wild animals such as leather, fur and ivory.

(iii) Collect honey without completely removing the beehives.

• Long Answer Type Questions

24. Describe the meaning and importance of sustainable development.

Ans. Sustainable development refers to the process of economic development where resources are used judiciously to satisfy needs of not only present generation but also to conserve them for the use of future generations. Sustainable development takes place without depleting the present natural resources.

The importance of sustainable development is discussed below

(i) It helps to conserve and make use of means and resources for the maximum benefit without wastage.

(ii) It awares the people about the responsibility to use and preserve natural resources.

(iii) It creates the feeling that natural resources are the common property of all and nobody can use the property according to his personal will. It helps to conserve natural and social environment.

(iv) People's participation is to be given priority in development work in order to achieve the aim of sustainable development.

(v) It attempts to create the concept of maintaining the present work for the future and conserving natural resources for future generation.

25. Describe any four major problems associated with sustainable development.

Ans. Four problems associated with sustained development are as follows

(i) The concept of sustainable development is subject to criticism. What, exactly, is to be sustained in a sustainable development? Any positive rate of exploitation of a non-renewable resource will eventually lead to exhaustion of Earth's final stock.

(ii) Turning the concept of sustainability into policy raises questions about how to assess the well-being of present and future generations. The issue is more complicated because our children do not just inherit environmental pollution and resource depletion, but also enjoy the fruits of our labour, in the forms of education, skills, and knowledge (i.e. human capital), as well as physical capital.

(iii) Poor management of natural resources, combined with growing economic activities, will continue to pose serious challenges to environment. The problem arises because people, institutions and governments have failed to evolve mechanism and policies to strike a balance between development and conservation of resources and preservation of environment.

(iv) The commonly held view that greater economic activity necessarily hurts the environment, is based on static assumptions about technology, tastes and environmental investments. In reality, the relationships between inputs and outputs and the overall effects of economic activities on the environment, are continually changing.

26. Mention the main principles of sustainable development.

Ans. Main principles of sustainable development are

(i) Respect and care for all forms of life.

(ii) Improving the quality of human life.

(iii) Minimising the depletion of natural resources.

(iv) Conserving the Earth's vitality and diversity.

(v) Enabling communities to care for their own environment.

(vi) Changing personal attitude and practices towards the environment.

27. Why is it important to adopt sustainable development? Explain.

Ans. A three-year study using satellites and aerial photography undertaken by the United Nations long ago warned that the environment had deteriorated so badly that it was 'critical' in many of eighty-eight countries, investigated. In view of all these findings and problems, sustainable development acquires much importance. Nature and mankind live and die together.

The Earth's vital signs reveal a patient in declining health. We need to realise our ethical and moral obligations to the mother Earth. Human beings are caretakers of the planet and responsible trustees of the legacy of future generations.

Due to the realisation of importance of sustainable development, now there is a transcending concern for survival of the people and planet. We need to take a holistic view of the very basis of our existence. The environmental problem does not necessarily signal our demise, rather it is our passport for the future. To save ourselves and our future generations from catastrophe, we require to take a holistic view, an ecological view, seeing the world as an integrated whole, rather than a dissociated collection of parts.

28. Mention some of the basic components of a green economy.

Ans. Some of the basic components of a green economy are as follows

(i) **Efficient and Sustainable Transport System** A green economy must have an efficient and sustainable public transport system. It should promote the use of cycles, carpools, public vehicles driven by green fuels, etc. to minimise the damage to the environment.

(ii) **Sustainable Industry** Sustainable industry uses improved processes to reduce, reuse and recycle water, raw materials, non-renewable minerals, energy, etc. It has an efficient waste disposal system that causes no damage to the environment and creates zero pollution.

(iii) **Sustainable Agriculture** In sustainable agriculture the production of crops takes place with the efficient use of resources without damaging the environment. Crop rotation, organic farming, use of bio-fertilizers and bio-pesticides, combining animal farming with crop farming are some examples of sustainable agricultural practices.

(iv) **Efficient Management of Land Resources** Land is used for farming, forests, factories, homes, roads, etc. In a green economy, land is used in such a way that it meets the requirements of people without causing damage to the environment.

Chapter Test

Multiple Choice Questions

1. What is sustainable development?
(a) Economic development at zero damage to ecology
(b) More and more development
(c) Development that meets the needs of present without endangering the ability of future generations to meet their needs.
(d) All of the above

2. Sustainable development requires proper use of
(a) natural resources
(b) man-made resources
(c) Both (a) and (b)
(d) human resources

3. The greatest problem related to sustainable development is to safeguard further depletion of which of the following?
(a) Fisheries and forests
(b) Croplands and grasslands
(c) Both (a) and (b)
(d) None of the above

4. The concept of 'sustainable development' became popular as the Brundtland Report in the year
(a) 1986
(b) 1987
(c) 1988
(d) 1990

5. To save water as a resources which techniques must be adopted?
(a) Rainwater harvesting
(b) Sprinkler irrigation
(c) Both (a) and (b)
(d) Recycling of waste

6. During the working lifetime of children born today, the population of the world will almost
(a) double
(b) triple
(c) destroy
(d) remain same

Short Answer Type Questions

7. Discuss the role of sustainable development to sustain biodiversity.

8. What are green buildings?

9. Why it is important to use renewable resources?

Long Answer Type Questions

10. What are the negative impact of human activities on the environment?

11. What are the goals of sustainable development?

Answers

Multiple Choice Questions

1. (c) *2. (c)* *3. (c)* *4. (b)* *5. (c)* *6. (a)*

For Detailed Solutions
Scan the code

CHAPTER 03

Database Management System

In this Chapter...

- Database Concept
- Database Management System (DBMS)
- Key Fields
- Data Storage
- Manipulating Data
- Creating a Database Object
- Creating a Table
- Building Forms
- Create and Manage Queries
- MySQL Command Basics
- Design Report

Database Concept

A database is a collection of logically related information/data, which is available for one or more users organised in a way, so that it can be easily accessed, managed and updated. It is actually a place, where related piece of information is stored and various operations can be performed on it by the user.

A database is basically a computer based record/data/information keeping system. Data is raw, unorganised facts and entities relevant to the user need to be processed such as a digital representation of text, numbers, graphical images or sound. The data are stored in such a way that, they are independent of the programs used by the people for accessing the data.

e.g. Consider the names, telephone numbers and addresses of the relatives, etc. You may have recorded this data in an indexed address book or you may have stored it on a hard drive, using application software such as Microsoft Access, OpenOffice.org BASE etc.

Database can be created with the help of following structures

Character → Field → Record → File → Database

Database Structure

Need for a Database

The need for a database arose in the early 1960s in response to the traditional file processing system. In the file processing system, the data is stored in the form of files and a number of application programs are written by programmers to add, modify, delete and retrieve data to and from appropriate files.

However, the file processing system has a number of problems, which are as follows

- Some information may be duplicate in several files.
- The file processing system lacks the insulation between program and data.
- Handling new queries is difficult, since it requires change in the existing application programs or requires a new application program.
- Unable to maintain data standards and does not provide data sharing.
- In this system, all the integrity rules need to be explicitly programmed in all application programs, which are using that particular data item.
- This system also lacks security features.

To overcome these problems, database system was designed.

Components of a Database

A database consists of several components. Each component plays an important role in the database system environment.

The major components of database are as follows

Data

It is raw numbers, characters or facts represented by value. Most of the organisations generate, store and process large amount of data. The data acts as a bridge between the hardware and the software. Data may be of different types such as User data, Metadata and Application Metadata.

Software

It is a set of programs that lies between the stored data and the users of database. It is used to control and manage the overall computerised database. It uses different types of software such as MySQL, Oracle, etc.

Hardware

It is the physical aspect of computer, telecommunication and database, which consists of the secondary storage devices such as magnetic discs, optical discs, etc., on which data is stored.

Users

It is the person, who needs information from the database to carry out its primary business responsibilities. The various types of users which can access the database system are as follows

(i) **Database Administrator (DBA)** A person, who is responsible for managing or establishing policies for the maintenance and handling the overall database management system is called DBA.

(ii) **Application Programmer** A person, who writes application programs in programming languages to interact and manipulate the database are called application programmer.

(iii) **End-user** A person, who interacts with the database system to perform different operations on the database like inserting, deleting, etc., through menus or forms is called end-user.

Features of a Database

Features of a database to let you manage your data are as follows

Tables

It is the building block of any relational database model, where all the actual data is defined and entered. A database consists of many tables. Tables (relations) consist of cells at the intersection of records (rows) and fields (columns). Different types of operations are done on the tables such as sorting, filtering, retrieving and editing of data. It is also known as a **file**.

(i) **Fields or Columns (Data item)** It is an area (within the record), reserved for a specific piece of data. It is the individual sub-component of one record. It contains set of characters. e.g. Customer number, customer name, street address, city, state, phone number, current address, date of birth, etc. Field in a table is also known as column or attribute.

(ii) **Records or Rows or Tuples** It is the collection of data items of all the fields (information) pertaining to one entity or a complete unit of information, i.e. a person, company, transition, etc. Record of a table is also known as row, entity or tuple.

Queries

It is an inquiry into the database using the SELECT statement. These statements give you filtered data according to your conditions and specifications indicating the fields, records and summaries which a user wants to fetch from a database.

It allows you to extract information from the database based on the conditions that you define in query. MS-Access 2007 supports the database object query.

Forms

In a database, a form is a window or a screen that contains numerous fields or spaces to enter data. Forms can be used to view and edit your data. It is an interface in user specified layout.

e.g. A user can create a data entry form that looks exactly like a paper form. People generally prefer to enter data into a well-designed form, rather than a table.

Reports

When you want to print those records which are fetched from your database, design a report. It is an effective way to present data in a printed format. It allows you to represent data retrieved from one or more tables, so that it can be analysed.

Database Server

The term database server may refer to both hardware and software used to run a database, according to the context. As software, a database server is the back end portion of a database application, following the traditional client server model.

Database Management System (DBMS)

It is a collection of programs that enables users to create, maintain database and control all the access to the database. It is a computer based record keeping system.

The primary goal of the DBMS is to provide an environment that is convenient and efficient for user to retrieve and store information. It acts as an interface between the application program and the data stored in the database.

DBMS is a software package that manages database. e.g. MySQL, INGRES, MS-Access, etc.

DBMS is actually a tool that is used to perform any kind of operation on data in database. It also maintains data consistency in case of multiple users. The purpose of a DBMS is to bridge the gap between information and data.

Some basic processes that are supported by a DBMS are as follows

- Specification of data types, structures and constraints to be considered in an application.
- Storing the data itself into persistent storage.
- Manipulation of the database.
- Querying the database to retrieve desired information.
- Updating the content of the database.

A short list of database applications would include:

- Inventory
- Payroll
- Membership
- Orders
- Shipping
- Reservation
- Invoicing
- Accounting
- Security
- Catalogues
- Mailing
- Medical records

Relational Database Management System (RDBMS)

RDBMS is a type of DBMS that stores data in the form of relations (tables). Relational databases are powerful, so they require few assumptions about how data is related or how it will be extracted from the databases.

An important feature of relational database system is that a single database can be spread across several tables. Base, Oracle, DB2, SAP, Sybase, ASE, Informix, Access, etc., are the examples of RDBMS.

Working of a Database

Database is created to operate large quantities of information by input, store, retrieve and manage the information. It is a centralised location which provides an easy way to access the data by several users. It does not keep the separate copies of a particular data file still a number of users can access the same data at the same time.

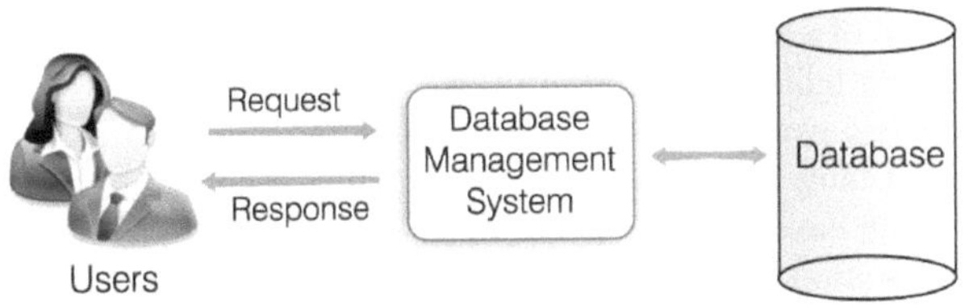

Working of a Database

As the diagram shows, DBMS works as an interface between the user and the centralised database. First, a request or a query is forwarded to a DBMS which works (i.e. a searching process is started on the centralised database) on the received query with the available data and if the result is obtained, it is forwarded to the user.

If the output does not completely fulfill the requirements of the user, then a rollback (again search) is done and again search process is performed until the desired output is obtained.

Advantages of a Database/DBMS

The centralised nature of database system provides several advantages, which overcome the limitations of the conventional file processing system. These advantages are as follows

(i) **Reduce Data Redundancy** Redundancy means 'duplication of data'. This eliminates the replication of data item in different files, extra processing required to face the data item from a large database. This also ensures data consistency and saves the storage space.

(ii) **Enforcing Data Integrity** It means that, the data contained in the database is accurate and consistent. Integrity constraints or consistency rules can be applied to database, so that the correct data can be entered into the database.

(iii) **Data Sharing** The data stored in the database can be shared among multiple users or application programs.

(iv) **Data Security** The DBMS ensures that the access of database is done only through an authorised user.

(v) **Ease of Application Development** The application programmer needs to develop the application programs according to the user's needs.

(vi) **Backup and Recovery** The DBMS provides backup and recovery sub-system that is responsible to recover data from hardware and software failures.

(vii) **Multiple Views of Data** A view may be the subset of database. Various users may have different views of the database itself.

(viii) **Enforced Standards** It can ensure that, all the data follow the applicable standards.

(ix) **Data Independence** System data descriptions are independent from the application programs.

Disadvantages of a Database/DBMS

There are many advantages of database, but database also have some minor disadvantages. These disadvantages are as follows

(i) **Cost of Hardware and Software** Through the use of a database system, new costs are generated due to additional hardware and software requirements.

(ii) **Complexity** A database system creates additional complexity and requirements.

(iii) **Database Failures** If database is corrupted due to power failure or it is corrupted on the storage media, then our valuable data may be lost or the system will stop working.

(iv) **Lower Efficiency** A database system is a multi-user software, which is less efficient.

- Data sharing refers to the process of sharing single piece of data among different users.
- Multiple mismatching copies of the same data is known as **data inconsistency**. If a field value is stored in two places in the database, then storage space is wasted and changing the data in one place will not cause data inconsistency.
- **Data redundancy** leads to data inconsistency.

Data Integrity

Data Integrity ensures the accuracy, reliability and consistency of the data during any operation.

Each type of data integrity are as follows

(i) **Entity Integrity** It defines the primary key of a table. Entity integrity rule on a column does not allow duplicate and null values.

(ii) **Domain Integrity** It defines the type, range and format of data allowed in a column. Domain integrity states that all values in a column must be of same type.

(iii) **Referential Integrity** It defines the foreign key concepts. Referential integrity ensures that data in related tables remains accurate and consistent before and after changes.

(iv) **User Defined Integrity** If there is some business requirements which do not fit any above data integrity then user can create own integrity, which is called user defined integrity.

Key Fields

The key is defined as the **column** or the set of columns of the database table which is used to identify each record uniquely in a relation. If a table has id, name and address as the column names, then each one is known as the **key** for that table. The key field is a unique identifier for each record.

e.g. In Student table, you could use a combination of the LastName and FirstName (or perhaps LastName, FirstName to ensure you to identify each student uniquely) as a key field.

Candidate Keys | Alternate Keys | Foreign Key | Primary Key

StudentId	FirstName	LastName	CourseId
L0002345	Jim	Black	C002
L0001254	James	Harradine	A004
L0002349	Amanda	Holland	C002
L0001198	Simon	McCloud	S042
L0023487	Peter	Murray	P301
L0018453	Anne	Norris	S042

Primary Key

Student table

CourseId	CourseName
A004	Accounts
C002	Computing
P301	History
S042	Short Course

Course table

Relationship between keys

Types of Key Fields

The following are the types of key fields available in the DBMS system

Primary Key

A field or a set of fields that uniquely identify each record in a table is known as a primary key. Each relation has atleast one column for which each row that must have a unique value. Only one column attribute can be defined as a primary key for each table.

A primary key must possess the following properties

- It does not allow null values.
- It has a unique index.
- It allows numbers and text both.

e.g. In the student's table, StudentId works as a primary key because it contains Ids which are unique for each student.

Note Data cannot be primary key.

Candidate Key

The set of all attributes which can uniquely identify each tuple of a relation are known as candidate keys. Each table may have one or more candidate keys and one of them will become the primary key. The candidate key of a relation is always a minimal key. e.g. Column StudentId and the combination of FirstName and LastName work as the candidate keys for the student table.

A candidate key must possess the following properties

- For each row, the value of the key must uniquely identify that row.
- No attribute in the key can be discarded without destroying the property of unique identification.

Alternate Key

From the set of candidate keys after selecting one of the keys as a primary key, all other remaining keys are known as alternate keys.

e.g. From the candidate keys (StudentId, combination of FirstName and LastName), if StudentId is chosen as a primary key, then the combination of FirstName and LastName columns work as alternate keys.

Foreign Key

A field of a table (relation) that references the primary key of another table is referred to as foreign key. The relationship between two tables is established with the help of foreign key. A table may have multiple foreign keys and each foreign key can have a different referenced table. Foreign keys play an essential role in database design, when tables are broken apart, then foreign keys make it possible for them to be reconstructed.

e.g. CourseId column of student table (reference table) works as a foreign key as well as a primary key for course table (referenced table).

Data Storage

A data type is a data storage format that can contain a specific type or range of values. The fields within a database often require a specific type of data to be input.

e.g. A school's record for a table student may use a character data type for the students first name and last name. The student's date of admission and date of birth would be stored in a date format, while his or her marks in each subject may be stored as a numeric.

In MS-Access, data types can be categorised into the following types

Data Types	Description
Text	Allows to store text or combination of text and numbers, as well as numbers that don't require calculations such as phone numbers. Also, it is a default data type.
Memo	Allows to store long blocks of text that use text formatting.
Number	Holds numeric values which are used for calculations and zip code. It includes various types such as Byte, Integer, Long Integer, (Single, Double) Replication ID and Decimal.
Date/Time	Allows to store date and time value for the year 100 to 9999.
Currency	Allows to store monetary values that can be used in calculations. Accurate upto 15 digits on LHS and 4 digits on RHS of decimal point.
AutoNumber	Allows to store numbers that are automatically generated for each record. It increases the number automatically when you add records.
Yes/No	Allows boolean value. (i.e. one of two possible values)
OLE Object	OLE is an acronym for Object Linking and Embedding. It can store objects such as a video clip, a picture, word document or any other binary data.
Hyperlink	Allows to store hyperlinks such as E-mail addresses.
Attachment	Allows to store files such as digital photos. Multiple files can be attached per record.
Lookup Wizard...	Lets you type a list of options, which can be chosen from a drop down list.

Field Length (Field Size)

It refers to the maximum number of characters that a field can contain. Each character requires one byte for its storage.

Field length is of two types which are as follows

(i) **Fixed Length Field** It is a type of field length in which the number of characters you enter in a field is fixed. These are present in Format option in Data Type Formatting group (in Datasheet tab) such as Currency, Euro, Per cent, etc.

(ii) **Variable Length Field** In this type of field length, the number of characters is not fixed. Actually, the number of characters of the data entered in the field decide the field length.

The field length or field size of each data type are as follows

Data Type	Field Length or Field Size	Data Type	Field Length or Field Size
Text	0-255 characters	Memo	0-65,536 characters
Number	1, 2, 4, 8 or 16 bytes	Date/Time	8 bytes
Currency	8 bytes	AutoNumber	4 or 16 bytes
Yes/No	1 bit (0 or 1)	OLE Object	Upto 2 GB
Hyperlink	Each part contains upto 2048 characters	Lookup Wizard...	4 bytes

Numeric Data Types

It allows the database server to store numbers such as integers and real numbers in a column.

e.g. Age of the students, numbers obtained in subjects, etc.

Types	Length in Bytes	Minimum Value (Signed)	Maximum Value (Signed)	Minimum Value (Unsigned)	Maximum Value (Unsigned)
TINYINT	1	– 128	127	0	255
SMALLINT	2	– 32768	32767	0	65535
MEDIUMINT	3	– 8388608	8388607	0	16777215
INT	4	– 2147483648	2147483647	0	4294967295
BIGINT	8	– 9223372036854775808	9223372036854775807	0	18446744073709551615

FLOAT (N, D) A small number with floating decimal point. It cannot be unsigned. Its size is 4 bytes. Here, N represents the total number of digits (including decimals) and 'D' represents the number of decimals.

DOUBLE (N, D) A large number with floating decimal point. It cannot be unsigned. Its size is 8 bytes.

DECIMAL (N, D) It cannot be unsigned. The maximum number of digits may be specified in the N parameter. The maximum number of digits to the right of the decimal point is specified in the D parameter.

String/Text Data Types

It allows the database server to store string values such as name of the Students, Address, etc.

Types	Description	Display Format	Range in Characters
CHAR	Contains non-binary strings. Length is fixed as you declare while creating a table. When stored, they are right-padded with spaces to the specified length.	Trailing spaces are removed	The length can be any value from 0 to 255.
VARCHAR	Contains non-binary strings. Columns are variable length strings. It contains alphanumeric value.	As stored	A value from 0 to 255 before MySQL 5.0.3.

Date and Time Data Types

It allows the database server to store a date using the fields YEAR, MONTH and DAY in the format YYYY-MM-DD. e.g. Date of admission, Date of birth, etc.

Types	Description	Display Format	Range
DATE	Use when you need only date information.	YYYY-MM-DD	'1000-01-01' to '9999-12-31'.
TIMESTAMP	Values are converted from the current time zone to UTC (Coordinated Universal Time) while storing and converted back from UTC to the current time zone when retrieved.	YYYY-MM-DD HH:MM:SS	'1970-01-01 00:00:01' UTC to '2038-01-19 03:14:07' UTC

Manipulating Data

In a database, structure and manipulation of data are done by some commands. For this, we can use SQL commands. SQL (Structured Query Language) commands are the instructions used to communicate with the database to perform specific task that work with data.

SQL commands can be used not only for searching the database but also to perform various other functions like, create tables, add data to tables, modify data, drop the tables, set permissions for users and many more.

Data Definition Language (DDL)

DDL is used to define the structure of your tables and other objects in the database. In DBMS, it is used to specify a database schema as a set of definitions (expressed in DDL). In SQL, the Data Definition Language allows you to create, alter and destroy database objects. Basically, a data definition language is a computer language used to create and modify the structure of database objects in a database. These database objects include views, schemes, tables, indexes, etc.

This term is also known as data description language in some contexts, as it describes the fields and records in a database table.

Data definition language consists of various commands that lets you to perform some specified tasks as follows

(i) **CREATE** Uses to create objects in the database.

(ii) **ALTER** Uses to alter the structure of the database table. This command can add up additional columns, drop existing columns and even change the data type of columns involved in a database table.

(iii) **DROP** Uses to delete objects from the database.

(iv) **TRUNCATE** Uses to remove all records from a table.

(v) **RENAME** Uses to rename an object.

Data Manipulation Language (DML)

DML provides various commands used to access and manipulate data in existing database. This manipulation involves inserting data into database tables, retrieving existing data, deleting data from existing tables and modifying existing data.

DML is mostly incorporated in SQL database. The basic goal of DML is to provide efficient human interaction with the system.

The DMLs are of two types

Procedural DMLs These require a user to specify what data is needed and how to get it.

Non-Procedural DMLs These require a user to specify what data is needed without specifying how to get it.

Various data manipulation language commands are as follows

(i) **SELECT** Used to retrieve data from a database.

(ii) **INSERT** Used to insert data into a table.

(iii) **UPDATE** Used to update existing data within a table.

(iv) **DELETE** Used to delete all records from a table, the space of the records remains.

(v) **LOCK TABLE** Used to control concurrency.

A query language is a portion of a DML involving information retrieval only. The terms DML and query language are often used synonymously.

Differences between DDL and DML

DDL	DML
DDL is the abbreviation of Data Definition Language.	DML is the abbreviation of Data Manipulation Language.
It is used to create and modify the structure of database objects in database.	It is used to retrieve, store, modify, delete, insert and update data in database.
DDL commands allow us to perform tasks related to data definition.	DML commands are used to manipulate data.
For example, CREATE, ALTER and DROP commands.	For example, SELECT, UPDATE and INSERT commands.

Transaction Control Language (TCL)

TCL is playing an important role in SQL. TCL commands are used to manage transactions in database. These are also used to manage the changes made by DML statements. It allows statements to be grouped together into logical transactions. A transaction is a single unit of work.
Each individual statement is a transaction. If a transaction is successful, all of the data modifications made during the transaction is committed and became a permanent part of the database. If a transaction encounters an error and must be cancelled or rolled back, then all of the data modifications are erased. To manage all these operations, transaction control language commands are used.

Various transaction control commands are as follows

(i) **COMMIT** Used to save the work done.

(ii) **SAVEPOINT** Used to identify a point in a transaction to which you can later rollback.

(iii) **ROLLBACK** Used to restore database to original, since the last COMMIT.

(iv) **SET TRANSACTION** It establishes properties for the current transactions.

Data Control Language (DCL)

DCL commands are used to assign security levels in database which involves multiple user setups. They are used to grant defined role and access privileges to the users.

There are two kinds of user in the schema

(i) **Users** They work with the data, but cannot change the structure of the schema. They write data manipulation language.

(ii) **Admin** They can change the structure of the schema and control access to the schema objects. They write data definition language.

Basically, the DCL component of the SQL language is used to create privileges that allow to users access and manipulation of the database.

Two types of DCL commands are

(i) **GRANT** Used to give user's access privileges to database.

(ii) **REVOKE** Used to withdraw access privileges given with the GRANT command.

Creating a Database Object

To create a new blank database, you need to perform the steps which are as follows

- Start **OpenOffice Base**, then getting started with its starting page will appear.

- Select create a new database under what do you want to do? and click on Next button.

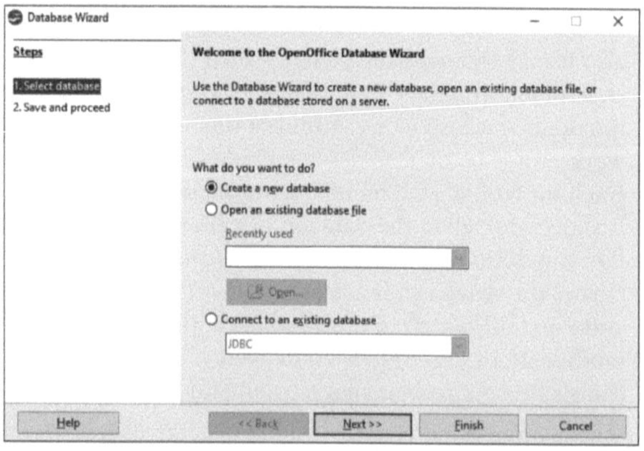

- Save and proceed window will appear. Click on Finish button.
- Now, SaveAs dialog box will appear where you can save your database with appropriate name. Click on Save button.

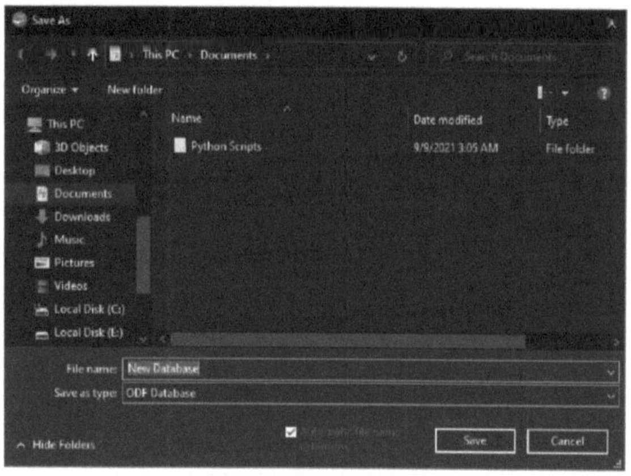

- Base creates the database with its features as Tables, Queries, Forms and Reports.

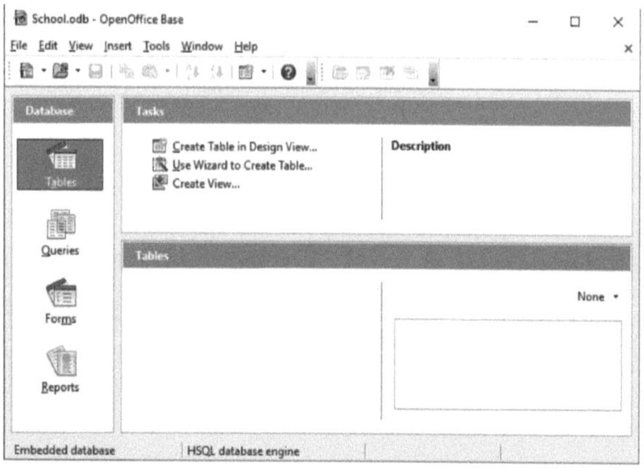

Creating Database Tables

To work with tables, click the Tables icon in the Database list. The three tasks that you can perform on a table are in the Task list

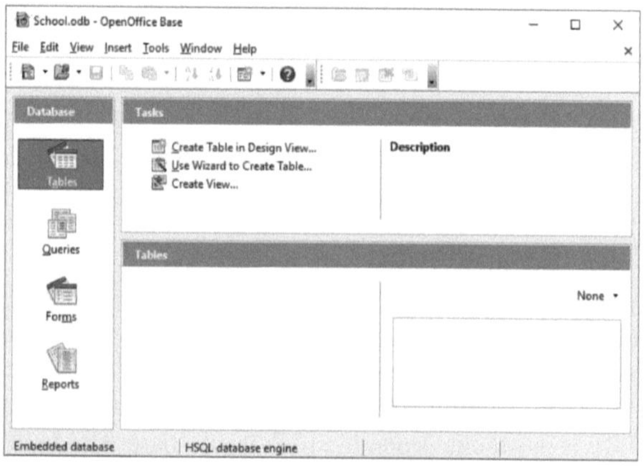

Creating Tables in Design View

Design View is a more advanced method for creating a new table. It allows you to directly enter information about each field in the table.

To create a table in design view, follow the given steps

- Open the Database.
- Select Create Table in Design View under Tasks. It will open a table as shown below

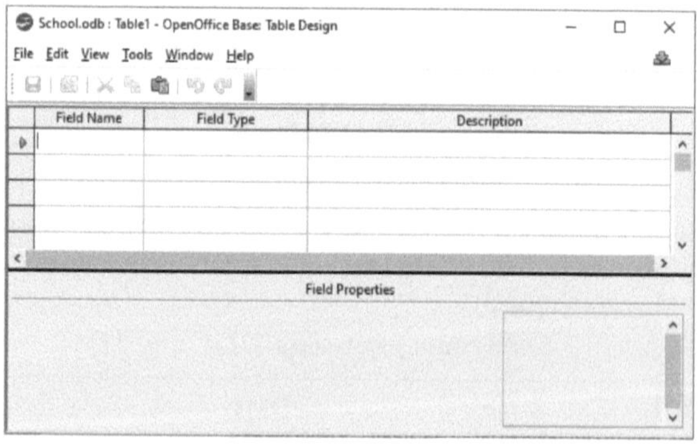

Note *The field entry area is used for entering field name, field type and description. This description is optional and the field properties pane is used for entering more details for each field, i.e. field size, validation rule etc. The table needs to be opened in Design View to access the field properties.*

Steps to add a new field are as follows

***Step* 1** Click on the first cell in the Field Name column and type the field name.

***Step* 2** Press Enter. The neighboring cell in the Field Type column is selected. To select the data type, click the drop-down arrow to the right of the Field Type field and select an alternative data type.

Step 3 Press Enter. A cell in the Description column will be selected. Enter a description, if required.

Step 4 Press Enter and repeat the above process for other fields.

Steps to set the field properties are as follows

Step 1 Click once on a Field Name for which you want to set the field property.

Step 2 The Field Properties will appear at the bottom of the screen as shown in the following figure

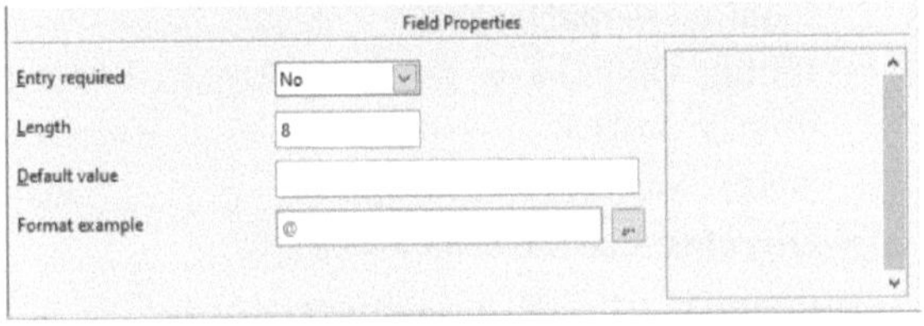

Here, you can set the properties of related field.

Make Changes in a Design View

The Design View of a table can be modified by the following changes

Insert a Field

Steps to insert a field in a table are as follows

Step 1 Select the field, before which you want to insert a new field.

Step 2 Right click at the selected field and click at the Insert Rows option from the context menu.

Step 3 A new field is added to the table design thus, you can enter field name, data type and description.

Delete a Field

Steps to delete a field from a table are as follows

Step 1 Select the field that you want to delete.

Step 2 Right click at the selected field and choose the option Delete from context menu.

Rename a Field

You can change a field name by placing the cursor on the field, double click on it and type the new name.

Naming and Saving of a Table

Steps to save a table are as follows

Step 1 To save the table, click the Save button at the top of the screen or click the File button and select Save. The Save As dialog box will appear as shown in following figure

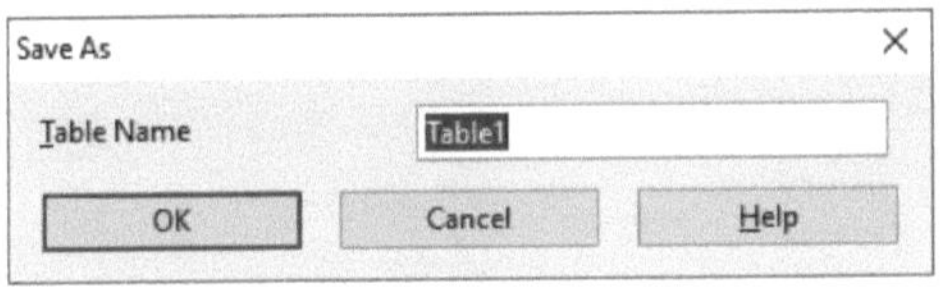

Step 2 Type the name that you want to give to your table in Table Name: text box.

Step 3 Click OK.

Entering/Removing Record into/from a Table

Once a table has been created, the field and its properties are defined, you can start to enter the records. This is done in a Datasheet View. If you create table in Design View, you need to switch to the Datasheet View to enter records.

Insert a Record

Steps to insert a record in a Datasheet View are as follows

Step 1 When you create a table, a new blank record automatically appears in the second row of the table or If you enter data in the last record, a new blank record will automatically appear at the end of the table.

Step 2 Type data into the fields.

Step 3 When you have finished adding records in the datasheet, save it and close it.

Delete an Existing Record

Steps to delete an existing record are as follows

Step 1 Select the row which you want to delete.

Step 2 Right click on the row and select the Delete from context menu.

Using the Wizard to Create a Table

To create a table using wizard, follow the below steps

- Open the database
- Select Use Wizard to Create Table under Tasks. It will open the Table Wizard as shown below

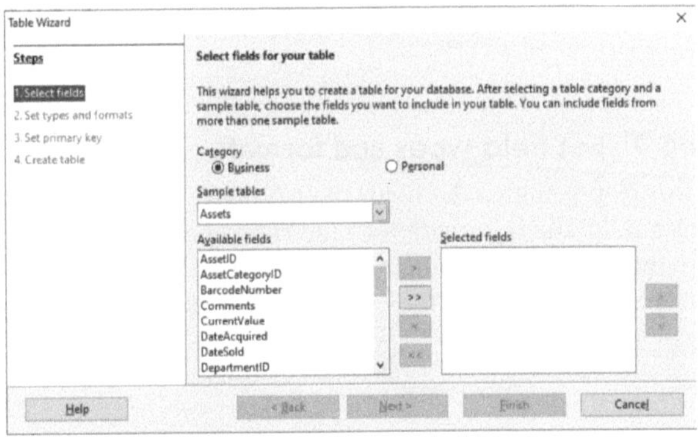

It has four steps as

Step 1 : Select fields

You have a choice of two categories of suggested tables: Business and Personal. Each category contains its own suggested tables from which to choose. Each table has a list of available fields. We will use the DVD-Collection Sample table in the Personal category to select the fields we need.

(i) **Category** Select Personal. The Sample Tables drop down list changes to a list of personal sample tables.

(ii) **Sample Tables** Select DVD-Collection. The Available fields window changes to a list of available fields for this table.

(iii) **Selected Fields** Using the > button, move these fields from the Available fields window to the Selected fields window in this order: CollectionID, MovieTitle, Actor, PurchasePrice, Rating, Notes Photo and Director.

(iv) Selected fields from another sample table. Click Business as the Category. Select Employees from the dropdown list of sample tables. Use the > button to move the Photo field from the Available fields window to the Selected fields window. It will be at the bottom of the list directly below the Director field.

(v) If a mistake is made in the order as listed above, click on the field name that is in the wrong order to highlight it. Use the Up or Down arrow on the right side of the Selected Fields list to move the field name to the correct position. Click Next.

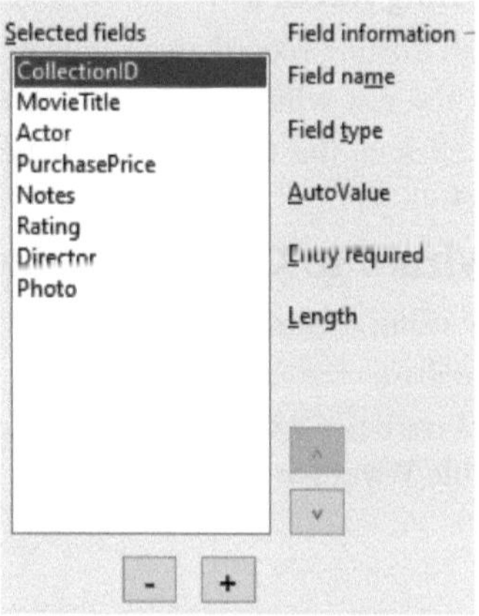

Step 2 : Set field types and formats

In this step you give the fields their properties. When you click a field, the information on the right changes. You can then make changes to meet your needs. Click each field, one at a time and make the changes listed below.

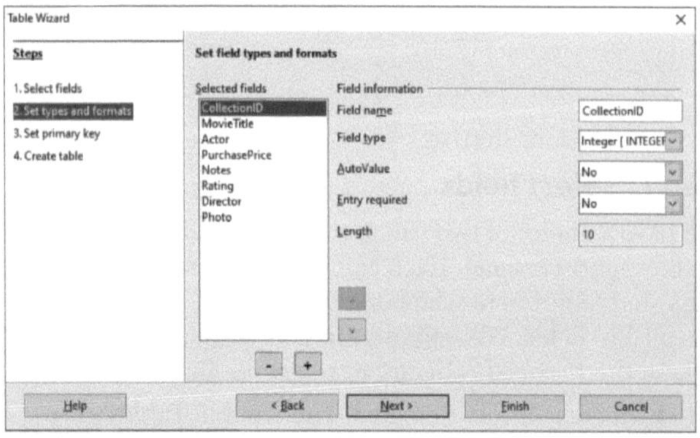

- **CollectionID** Change AutoValue from No to Yes.
- **MovieTitle** Default

(a) **Entry required** If all of your music is in albums, change Entry required to Yes. Otherwise, leave Entry required as No.

(b) **Length** Unless you have an album title that exceeds 100 characters in length counting the spaces, do not change the length.

- **Actor** Use the Default setting. And since music has authors, set Entry Required to Yes.
- **PurchasePrice** Length: default setting. Entry required should be Yes.
- **Rating** Only change the Entry Required setting: from No to Yes.
- **Notes** No changes are required.
- **Director** Use the default settings.
- **Photo** Use the default settings.

When you have finished, click Next.

Step 3: Set primary key

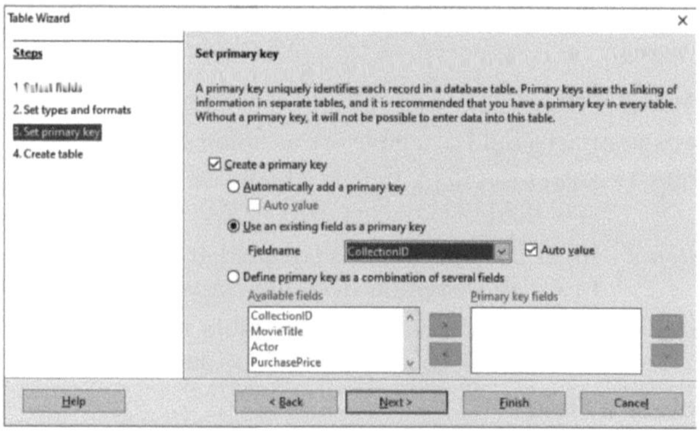

- Create a primary key should be checked.
- Select option Use an existing field as a primary key.
- In the Fieldname drop down list, select CollectionID.
- Check Auto value, if it is not already checked.
- Click Next.

Step 4 : Create the table

- If desired, rename the table at this point. If you rename it, make the name meaningful to you.
- Leave the option Insert data immediately checked.
- Click Finish to complete the table wizard. Close the window created by the table wizard.

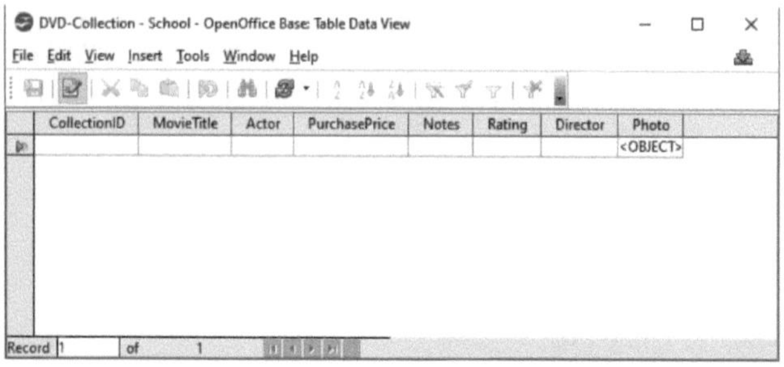

Creating a Table by Copying an Existing Table

If you have a large collection of music, you might want to create a table for each type of music you have. Rather than creating each table from the wizard, you can make a copy of the original table. Each table can be named according to the type of music contained in it. Possible names could include Classical, Pop, Country and Western, and Rock, among others.

- Click on the Tables icon in the Database pane to see the existing tables.
- Right-click on the DVD-Collection table icon. Select Copy from the context menu.
- Move the mouse pointer below this table, right-click and select Paste from the context menu. The Copy table window opens.
- Change the table name to Pop and click Next.
- Click the >> button to move all the Fields from the left window to the right window and click Next.
- Since all the Fields already have the proper File Type formatting, no changes should be needed. Click Create. The new table is created.

Opening an Existing Table

Existing table can be opened by following steps

Step 1 Find a table in the All Base Objects list (the right hand window).

Step 2 Right click on a table and select Open. This view represents the data in a table.

Renaming and Deleting a Table

Steps to rename a table are as follows

Step 1 Find a table in the All Base Objects list (the left hand window).

Step 2 Right click on a table and select Rename from context menu that appears.

Step 3 Now, type a new name for the table.

Step 4 Press Enter from the keyboard.

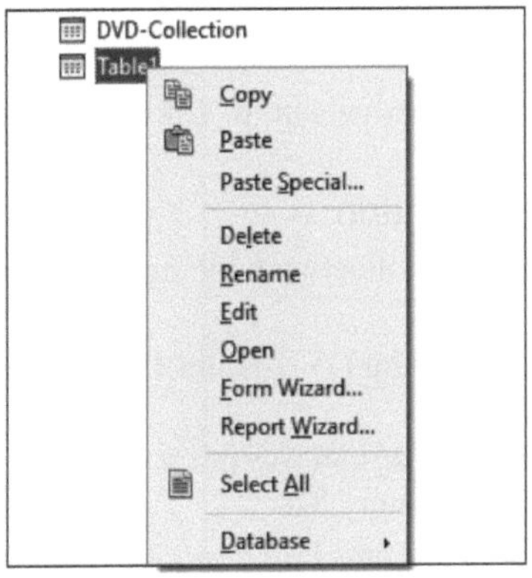

Steps to delete a table are as follows

Step 1 Find a table in the All Base Objects list.

Step 2 Right click on a table and select Delete.

Step 3 Now, OpenOffice Base will display the prompt message to confirm that you want to delete the table or not.

Step 4 Click on Yes button to delete a table with its contents.

Building Forms

Forms are used for entering, modifying and viewing records you likely have had to fill out forms on many occasions, like when visiting a doctor's clinic, applying for a job or registering for school. When you enter information in a form in Base, the data goes exactly where the database designer wants it to go: in one or more related tables.

There are two ways to create forms in Base

Using the Wizard to Create a Form

In the main database window, click the Form icon. Double click Use Wizard to Create Form to open the wizard.

Follow the below steps to create a form using wizard

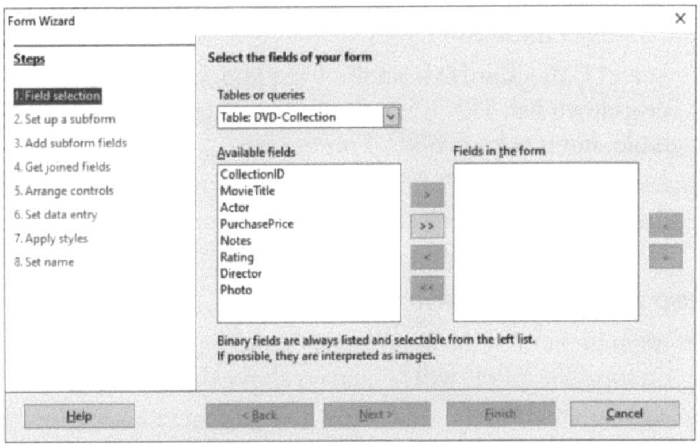

Step 1 : Field selection

- Under Tables or queries, select DVD-Collection as the table. Available fields lists the fields for the DVD-Collection table.
- Click the right double arrow to move all of these fields to the Fields in the form list. Click Next.

Step 2: Set up a subform

Since, we have not already created a relationship between the Table1 and DVD-Collection tables. If no relationship had been defined, this would be done in step 4.

- Click the box labeled Add Subform.
- Click the radio button labeled Subform based on manual selection of fields.
- Click Next.

Step 3 : Add subform fields

This step is exactly the same as step 1. The only difference is that not all of the fields will be used in the subform.

- Select Table1 under Tables or queries.
- Use the >> button to move all the fields to the right.

- Click the ID field to highlight it.
- Use the < button to move the ID to the left.
- Click Next.

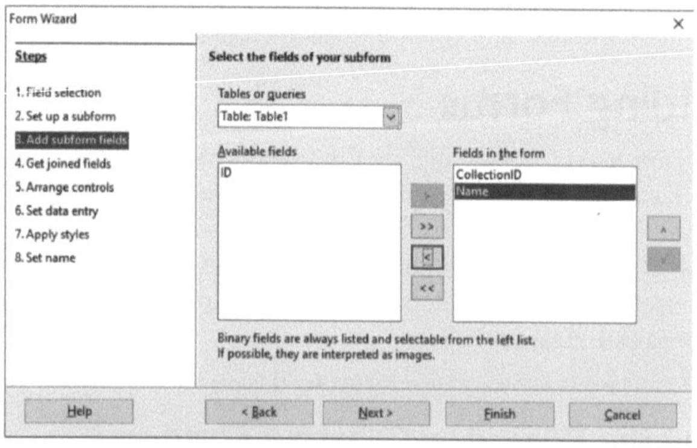

Step 4 : Get joined fields

This step is for tables or queries for which no relationship has been defined. Since we want to list all expenses by the day they occur in both the form and subform, we will join the Date fields of these two tables

- Select CollectionID from the First joined subform field dropdown list. This is not the Primary key for the Table1 table, but it is known as a Foreign key.
- Select CollectionID from the First joined main form field dropdown list. This is the Primary key for the DVD-Collection table. Click Next.

Step 5 : Arrange controls

- Arrangement of the main form: Click Columnar - Labels on top. The labels will be placed above their field.
- Arrangement of the subform: Click As Data Sheet. (The labels are column headings and the field entries are in spreadsheet format.)

  Click Next.

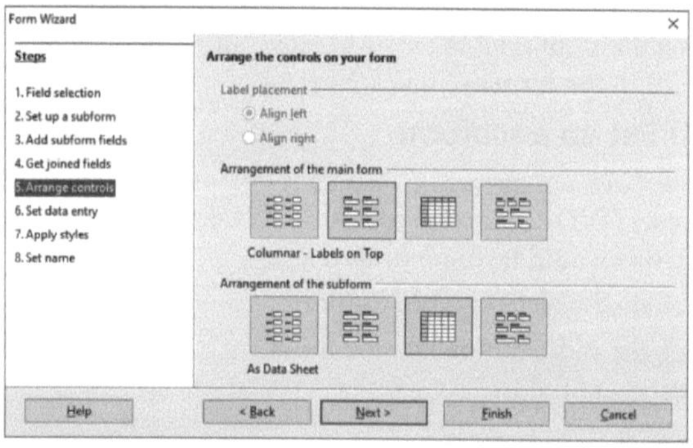

Step 6 : Set data entry

Unless you have a need for any of these entries to be checked, accept the default settings. Click Next.

Step 7 : Apply styles

- Select the color you want in the Apply Styles list.
- Select the Field border you want.
- Click Next.

Step 8: Set name

- Enter the name for the form. In this case, it is DVD.
- Click the circle in front of Modify the form if you want to modify the form otherwise select first option.
- Click Next. The form opens in Edit mode, if you select Modify the form.

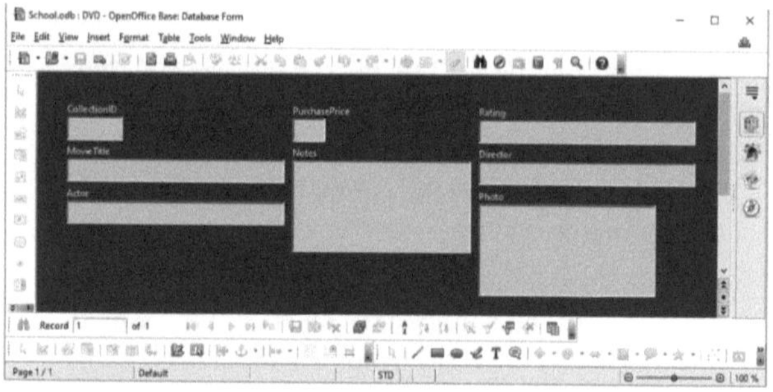

2. Creating forms in Design View

To create a form using design view, follow below steps

- In the main database window, click the Form icon. Double click Create Form in Design View.
- It will open the base form where you can design your form with the help of form controls which are given in left side of form window.

Create and Manage Queries

Queries are the basis of power in a database. It is a way to get specific information from the database. They give us the ability to ask questions, record the questions for later and to take actions on the answers. There are two methods for creating a query in OpenOffice Base. These are as follows

Using the Wizard to Create a Query

In the main database window , click the Queries icon in the Databases section, then in the Tasks section, click Use Wizard to Create Query.

The Query Wizard window opens. Now follow the below steps

Step 1 : Field selection

- Select the DVD-Collection table from the dropdown list of tables.
- Select fields from the DVD-Collection table in the Available fields list.
  (a) Click MovieTitle, and use the > button to move it to the Fields in Query list.
  (b) Move the Actor and PurchasePrice fields in the same manner.
  (c) Use the up arrow to change the order of the fields.
  (d) Click Next.

Step 2 : Sorting order

Up to four fields can be used to sort the information of our query.

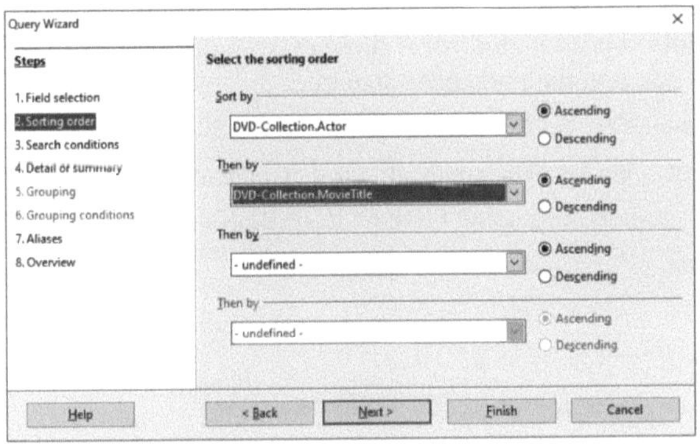

- Click the first Sort by dropdown list.
  - (a) Click DVD-Collection.Actor to select it.
  - (b) If you want the actors to be listed in alphabetical order (a-z), select Ascending on the right. If you want the artist listed in reverse order (z-a), select Descending on the right.
- Click the second Sort by dropdown list.
  - (a) Click DVD-Collection.MovieTitle.
  - (b) Select Ascending or Descending according to the order you want.
- Repeat this process for DVD-Collection. Purchase Price.
- Click Next.

Step 3 : Search conditions

The search conditions available are listed below. They allow us to compare the name we entered with the names of the actor in our database and decide whether to include a particular actor in our query or not.

- Since we are only searching for one thing, we will use the default setting of Match all of the following.
- We are looking for a particular actor, so select is equal to.
- Enter the name of the actor in the Value box. Click Next.

Step 4 : Detail or summary

We want simple information, so the default setting: Detailed query is what we want. Click Next.

Step 5 : Aliases

We want the default settings. Click Next.

Step 6 : Overview

- Name the query.
- To the right of this are two choices. Select Display Query.
- Click Finish.

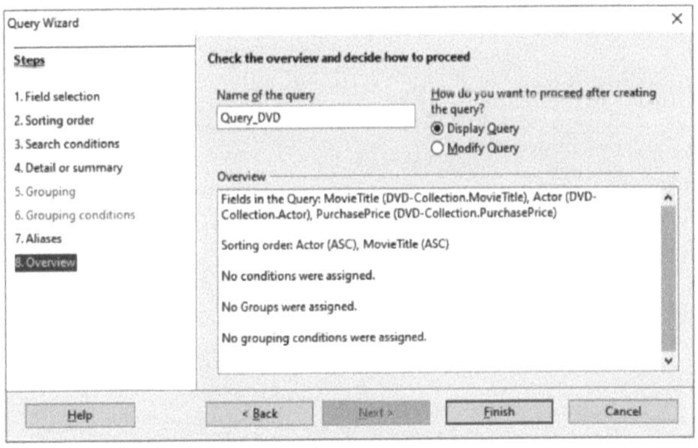

Using the Design View to Create a Query

OpenOffice Base provides you the functionality to create a query by using a Design View.

Steps to create a query through a Design View are as follows

Step 1 In the main database window , click the Queries icon in the Databases section, then in the Tasks section, click Create Query in Design View.

Step 2 The Add Table or Query dialog box will appear as shown in the following figure

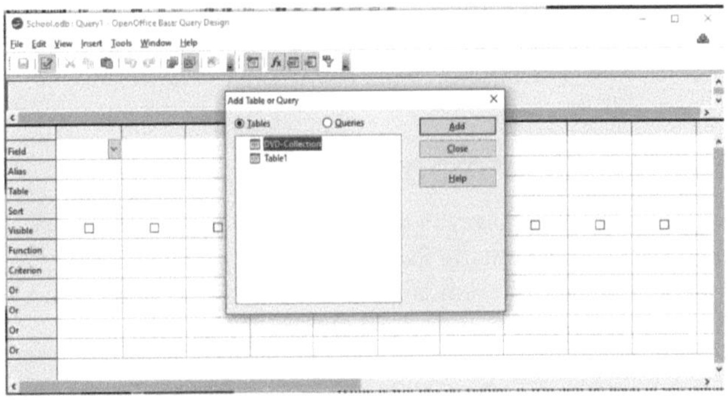

Step 3 Select a table in the Tables tab and click the Add button to add a table.

Step 4 The selected table is being displayed as shown in the following figure. You can click the Close button to close the Add Table or query dialog box.

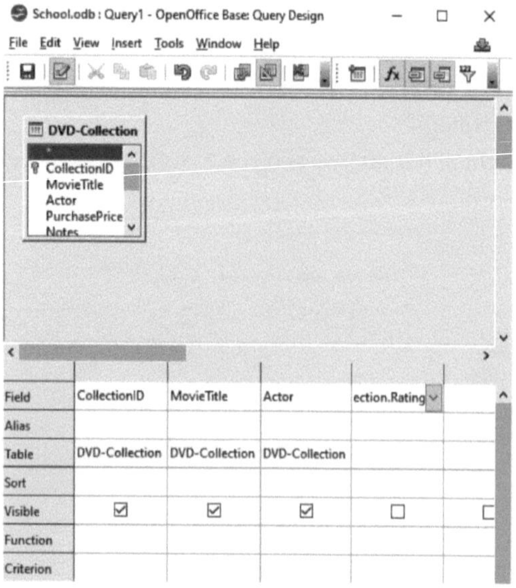

Step 5 Edit the Field row and other rows.

Step 6 Save the query by using shortcut Ctrl+ S key. The SaveAs dialog box will appear, enter the name of your query in Query Name text field and then, click OK button.

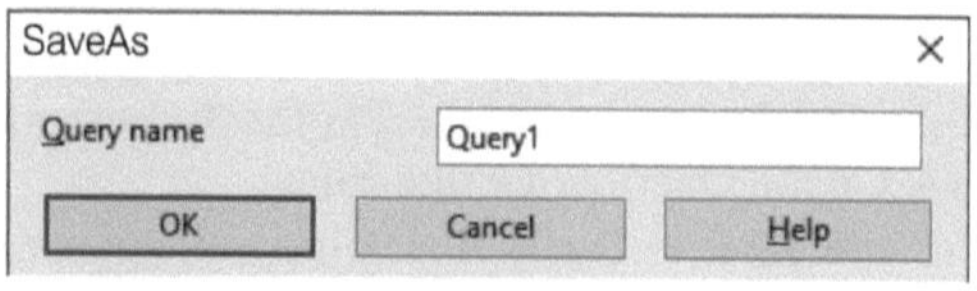

Step 7 Select the Run Query from standard toolbar or press F5 from keyboard.

Step 8 The query will display the output in a tabular form.

MySQL Command Basics

MySQL database is a way of organizing a group of tables and table stores the data in the form of rows and columns. To create a bunch of different tables that share a common theme, you would group them into one database to make the management process easier. So, for manipulating data, we need to know about MySQL commands, which are described below.

CREATE Command

Create a database Creating database is an easier task. You need to just type the name of the database in a CREATE DATABASE command.

Syntax

```
CREATE DATABASE [IF NOT EXISTS]<database_name>;
```

CREATE DATABASE command will create an empty database with the specified name and would not contain any table.

IF NOT EXISTS is an optional part of this statement which prevents you from an error if there exists a database with the given name in the database catalogue.

For example, `mysql>CREATE DATABASE BOOK;`

Output Query OK, 1 row affected <0.01 sec>

Tables are created using CREATE TABLE command.

Syntax

```
CREATE TABLE table_name
(
        column_name1 data_type(size),
        column_name2 data_type(size),
        ------
);
```

Here,

CREATE TABLE defines a new table.

table_name defines the name of a table.

column_name defines the name of a column.

data_type specifies that which type of data can be contained in a particular column.

For example,

```
mysql > CREATE TABLE STUDENT (Student_Code
integer, Student_Name char(20), Sex char(1),
Grade char(2), Total_Marks decimal);
```

Output

```
Query OK, 0 row affected <0.06 sec>
```

Some rules for creating tables are as follows

- The table and column names must start with a letter and can be followed by letters, numbers, or underscores.
- Table or column names not to exceed a total of 30 characters in length and not use any SQL reserved keywords as names for tables or column names (such as 'select', 'create', 'insert', etc).
- It is important to make sure that you are using an open parenthesis before the beginning of a table definition and a closing parenthesis after the end of the last column definition.
- Separate each column definition with a comma (,).
- All SQL statements should end with a semi-colon (;).

INSERT Command

The INSERT command is used to add a single record or multiple records into a table.

Syntax

```
INSERT INTO <table_name>(col_1, col_2,
col_3,..., col_n) VALUES(value_1, value_2,...
value_n);
```

Here,

`table_name` defines the name of a table where data will be inserted.

`col_1, col_2, col_3,..., col_n` are the columns of the current table.

`value_1, value_2,... value_n` are the data values against each column.

For example, The following information exists in the table STUDENT

Roll No	Name	Subject
101	Rahul	Art
102	Vikas	Science
103	Puneet	Science
104	Sachin	Art
105	Uday	Commerce

To add a new row into the STUDENT table use the INSERT command as follow

```
mysql>INSERT INTO STUDENT(Roll_No, Name,
Subject) VALUES(106, 'Ajay', 'Science');
```

Now, the table STUDENT will look like as follows

Roll_No	Name	Subject
101	Rahul	Art
102	Vikas	Science
103	Puneet	Science
104	Sachin	Art
105	Uday	Commerce
106	Ajay	Science

SELECT Command

The most commonly used SQL command is SELECT statement. The SQL SELECT statement is used to query or retrieve data from a table in the database. A query may retrieve information from specified columns or from all of the columns in the table.

Syntax

```
SELECT column_list
FROM table_name;
```

Selecting Specific Columns

To select any specific column or information from the table, we use the following command:

Syntax

```
SELECT<column_name1>,[<column_name2>,…,<column_
nameN>] FROM <table_name>;
```

Example To display the column Emp_Code and Emp_Salary from table COMPANY

Company

Emp_Code	Emp_ Name	Emp_Salary	Emp_Dep	Joining_Date
101	Ravi	28000	D02	2010-10-10
102	Neeru	70000	D03	2013-06-04
103	Shrey	60000	D05	2011-03-02
104	Puneet	15000	D07	2009-05-01
105	Sneha	12000	D08	2008-04-03

```
mysql>SELECT Emp_Code, Emp_Salary FROM COMPANY;
```

Output

Emp_Code	Emp_Salary
101	28000
102	70000
103	60000
104	15000
105	12000

Selecting All Columns

To select all the columns of a table or entire table, we can use an asterisk (*) symbol in place of column_name list.

Syntax

```
SELECT * FROM <table_name>;
```

Example To display all the columns of table COMPANY.

```
mysql>SELECT * FROM COMPANY;
```

Output

It will display the complete table COMPANY.

UPDATE Command

The UPDATE command is used to update a single record or multiple record in a table. The UPDATE command is used to modify the existing rows in a table.

Syntax

```
UPDATE<table_name > SET <column1> = <value1>,
<column2> = <value2> ,.....
WHERE <condition>;
```

Example To update Emp_Salary with 28000 of those employees whose Emp_Code is 100.

```
mysql> UPDATE COMPANY SET Emp_Salary=28000
              WHERE Emp_Code=100;
```

The above query will update the Emp_Salary by 28000 whose Emp_Code is 100.

DELETE Command

To discard unwanted data from a database, the DELETE command is used. The DELETE command uses a WHERE clause.

If you don't use a WHERE clause, all rows in the table will be deleted.

Syntax

```
DELETE FROM <table_name> WHERE <condition>;
```

Example To delete the record of employee Puneet from the table COMPANY.

```
mysql>DELETE FROM COMPANY
           WHERE Emp_Name ='Puneet';
```

The above query will delete the record of Puneet from table COMPANY

Delete All Rows To delete all rows in a table without deleting the table structure, the following command is used.

Syntax DELETE FROM<table–name>;

Example To delete all rows from table COMPANY.

```
mysql>DELETE FROM COMPANY;
```

The above query will delete all data of table COMPANY.

Design Report

Report offers you the ability to present your data in print. Reports are useful because they allow you to present components of your database in easy to read format.

To create a new report, follow the below steps

- Click the Reports icon in the Database list.
- In the Tasks list, click Use Wizard to Create Report. The Report Wizard window opens.

Step 1 : Field selection

- Select Table: DVD-Collection in the Tables or Queries dropdown list.
- Use the > to move these fields from the Available fields list to the Fields in report list. Click Next.

Step 2: Labeling fields

- Click the field label you want to change and make your changes as you would in any text box.
- Click Next.

Step 3 : Grouping

Since we are grouping by the date, use the > button to move the Date field to the Groupings list. Click Next.

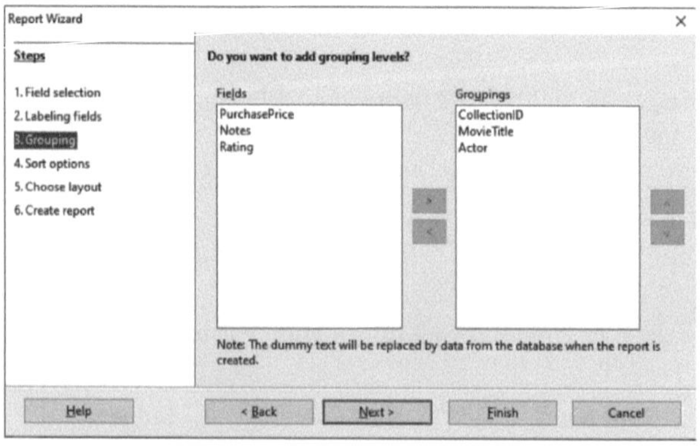

Step 4 : Sort options

We do not want to do any additional sorting. Click Next.

Step 5 : Choose layout

We will be using the default settings for the layout. Click Next.

Step 6 : Create report

- Label the report: DVD Report
- Select Static report.
- Click Finish.

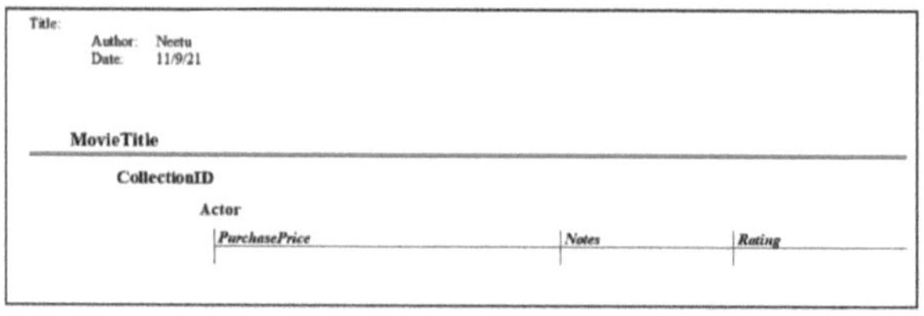

Printing a Report

To print a report, follow the given steps

(i) You can print the report by clicking on Print command from File tab or press Ctrl + P from keyboard.

(ii) Print dialog box will appear on the screen.

(iii) Here, you can set your printer and click on Print button.

Chapter Practice

PART 1
Objective Questions

• Multiple Choice Questions

1. Databases have the ability to
(a) store a large amount of data in a structured format, easy update, sort query, production of reports
(b) spell check, perform calculations, library of mathematical functions, replication
(c) rotate images, copy and paste, fill scale
(d) None of the above

Ans. (*a*) Databases have the ability to store a large amount of data in a structured format, easy update, sort query, production of reports.

2. Which of the following is not an example of database?
(a) Cross knot game
(b) Employee payroll management
(c) Numeric calculator
(d) Customer management system

Ans. (*c*) Numeric calculator because it is used to calculate the numeric numbers only. This application is unable to store data in it.

3. Database is a combination of
(a) hardware and software
(b) hardware and operating system
(c) software and operating system
(d) utility programs

Ans. (*a*) A database consists of several components. These are data, software, hardware and user.

4. Operations performed on a databases are controlled by
(a) user (b) hardware (c) DBMS (d) RDBMS

Ans. (*a*) Users are those persons, who need the information from the database to perform operations.

5. Which of the following is not a component of a database?
(a) tables (b) queries (c) forms (d) formula bar

Ans. (*d*) Database is made up of tables, queries, forms and reports.

6. All the information about a thing or a person is known as a
(a) database (b) file
(c) field (d) record

Ans. (*d*) A record refers to a row of data which represents a complete set of information in a table.

7. Out of the following, which one is the most appropriate data field in context of employee table, if only one of these is required?
(a) Age in years
(b) Data of birth
(c) Age in days
(d) Age in months

Ans. (*b*) Date of birth is the most appropriate data field in context of employee table.

8. Which of the following is not the main building block of a database?
(a) Lists (b) Queries
(c) Reports (d) Forms

Ans. (*a*) The main building blocks of database are tables, queries, forms and reports.

9. Which of the following best describes a form?
(a) Form enables people to enter or view data in a database easily.
(b) Form summarises and prints data.
(c) A form filters data from a database based on a criteria
(d) All of the above

Ans. (*a*) Form enables people to enter or view data in a database easily. Forms allow you to add, update and delete the data in the database one-by-one.

10. DBMS is a program that controls the creation, maintenance and use of database. Here, DBMS referred to
(a) Digital Base Management System
(b) Data Build Management System
(c) Database Management System
(d) Database Management Service

Ans. (*c*) Here, DBMS stands for Database Management System.

11. Computer based record keeping system is known as
(a) Data Manipulation System
(b) Computerised Data System
(c) Computerised Record Keeping System
(d) DBMS

Ans. (*d*) DBMS is a collection of programs that enable user to create and maintain database. Also , it is a computer based record keeping system.

12. RDBMS provides relational operators to manipulate the data. Here, RDBMS refers to
(a) Record Database Management System
(b) Relational Database Management System
(c) Reference Database Management System
(d) None of the above

Ans. (*b*) RDBMS stands for Relational Database Management System which provides operator to manipulate the data stored into the database table.

13. A database that contains tables linked by common fields is called a
(a) Centralised database
(b) Flat file database
(c) Relational database
(d) None of the above

Ans. (*c*) Relational database stores data in the form of tables which are linked by common fields.

14. Duplication of data is known as
(a) data security
(b) data incomplete
(c) data redundancy
(d) None of the above

Ans. (*c*) Data redundancy means duplication of data. It eliminates replication of data item into different files from a large database.

15. Key field is a unique identifier for each record. It is defined in the form of
(a) rows
(b) columns
(c) tree
(d) query

Ans. (*b*) Key is a data item that allows you to uniquely identify individual occurrences which is defined as the column or set of columns.

16. Which of the following fields will not make a suitable primary key?
(a) A customer's account number
(b) A data field
(c) An auto number field
(d) A student's admission number

Ans. (*b*) From the given options, data field cannot be set as a primary key because it cannot be fixed for an object.

17. When you define a field for a table, which of the following parameters do access always consider optional?
(a) Field Name (b) Data Type
(c) Field Size (d) Description

Ans. (*d*) Description field of table is optional, as it depends on database designer that he/she wants to describe field or not.

18. The design of the database is known as
(a) attribute (b) database scheme
(c) abstraction (d) database oriented

Ans. (*b*) Database schema is the logical representation of data which shows how the data is stored logically in the entire database.

19. A relational database is a collection of
(a) attributes (b) tables
(c) records (d) fields

Ans. (*b*) In a relational database, all data is arranged in tables, which are made up of rows and columns.

20. A tuple in RDBMS is referred to .... of a table.
(a) record (b) field
(c) table (d) key

Ans. (*a*) A single row of a table, that contains a single record for that relation is called a tuple.

21. .... refers to the attribute that can uniquely identify tuples within the relation.
(a) Foreign key (b) Consolidate key
(c) Alternate key (d) Primary key

Ans. (*d*) A primary key in a table is a column or a group of columns that uniquely identify every row in that table. The primary key cannot be a duplicate, i.e. the same value cannot appear more than once in the table. e.g. Student's roll number, Product ID etc.

22. Which of the following is an attribute whose value is derived from the primary key of some other table?
(a) Primary key (b) Foreign key
(c) Alternate key (d) None of these

Ans. (*b*) A foreign key is a column or a group of columns in a relational database table that provides a link between data in two tables.

• Case Based MCQs

Direction *Read the case and answer the following questions.*

23. Mr. Amar Agarwal is the owner of his parental firm Agarwal & Sons which deals in the wholesale business of spices.

He wants to maintain records of spices available in their shop and generate bills when someone purchases any spices from the shop. They want to create a database to keep track of all the spices in the shop and the spices purchased by customers.

(i) Which is the correct SQL statement to create the table?

(a) CREATE TABLE spice(scode integer, sname char(25), price decimal, stock integer)

(b) CREATE spice(scode integer, sname char(25), price decimal, stock integer)

(c) CREATE spice(scode , sname , price, stock)

(d) SELECT TABLE spice(scode integer, sname char(25), price decimal, stock integer)

(ii) To add records in the table which of the following SQL statement is used?

(a) ADD (b) SELECT

(c) INSERT (d) INSERT INTO

(iii) To add a new column exp_date in the existing table the statement is

(a) ALTER TABLE spice ADD (exp_date date);

(b) UPDATE TABLE spice ADD (exp_date date);

(c) MODIFY spice ADD (exp_date date);

(d) ALTER TABLE spice MODIFY (exp_date date);

(iv) To view the table structure of the above created table the command is

(a) SELECT spice

(b) DESC spice

(c) DESCRIBE spice

(d) Both (b) and (c)

(v) To create an index on name of spices in the existing table, the command is

(a) ALTER TABLE spice ADD INDEX spice_idx (sname)

(b) CREATE INDEX spice_idx ON spice (sname)

(c) CREATE TABLE spice (INDEX spice_idx (sname))

(d) Both (a) and (b)

Ans. (i) (*a*) CREATE TABLE is an SQL command to define a new table.

(ii) (*d*) The INSERT INTO statement adds new rows/ tuples to the table. The order of values matches the order of column names in the table.

(iii) (*a*) To add a new column in an existing table following syntax is used :

```
ALTER TABLE <table_name> ADD
<column_name> <data type> <size>
[constraint name];]
```

Hence, to add a new column exp_date in the existing table the statement is

```
ALTER TABLE spice ADD (exp_date date);
```

(iv) (*d*) To view the table structure DESCRIBE spice command is used.

(v) (*d*) Index can be created using one of the following methods

- CREATE INDEX <index_name> ON <table_name> (col1, col2...)
- ALTER TABLE <table_name> ADD INDEX <index_name> (col1, col2....)

24. Consider the table STUDENT with following details.

Table : STUDENT

STU_ID	Name	Stream	Marks	Class
1	Armaan	Science	87.5	12A
2	Vicky	Commerce	88.7	12B
3	Meeta	Humanities	76.8	12C
4	Vanisha	Science	79.5	12A
5	Kanika	Science	77.9	12A
6	Anandi	Commerce	86.7	12B

(i) Command to select all Commerce students from the table STUDENT.

(a) SELECT * FROM STUDENT;

(b) SELECT Stream FROM STUDENT WHERE Stream= 'Commerce';

(c) SELECT * FROM STUDENT WHERE Stream = 'Commerce';

(d) SELECT Name FROM STUDENT WHERE Stream = 'Commerce';

(ii) View all records other than '12A' class.

(a) SELECT DISTINCT Class FROM STUDENT;

(b) SELECT Class FROM STUDENT WHERE (Class NOT = 'Science');

(c) SELECT * FROM STUDENT WHERE Class NOT IN ('Science');

(d) None of the above

(iii) Modify the marks of Kanika as 85.5.

(a) ALTER TABLE STUDENT SET Marks = 85.5 WHERE Name = 'Kanika';

(b) UPDATE STUDENT SET Marks=85.5 WHERE Name = Kanika';

(c) UPDATE TABLE STUDENT SET Marks =85.5 WHERE Name= 'Kanika';

(d) ALTER STUDENT SET Marks=85.5 WHERE Name = 'Kanika';

(iv) Command to delete all records that belongs to 'Science' stream .

(a) DELETE FROM STUDENT WHERE Stream= 'Science';

(b) DROP FROM STUDENT WHERE Stream= 'Science';

(c) DROP TABLE STUDENT WHERE Stream= 'Science';

(d) None of the above

(v) Add a record of new student 'Rashmi' of 'Humanities' stream in class '12B' and her marks is '70.9'.

(a) `INSERT INTO STUDENT VALUES ('Rashmi', 'Humanities', '12B', 70.9);`
(b) `INSERT INTO STUDENT VALUES (7,'Rashmi', 'Humanities', '12B', 70.9);`
(c) `INSERT INTO STUDENT VALUES ('Rashmi', 'Humanities', 70.9, '12B');`
(d) `INSERT INTO STUDENT VALUES (7,'Rashmi', 'Humanities', 70.9, '12B');`

Ans. (i) (*c*) Command to select all Commerce students from the table STUDENT is

```
SELECT*FROM STUDENT WHERE Stream=
'Commerce';
```

(ii) (*d*) Here, none of the query statisfies the given condition. To solve the query SELECT statement should have been used. The correct statement is

```
SELECT*FROM STUDENT WHERE CLASS NOT IN
('12A');
```

(iii) (*b*) Command to modify the marks of Kanika as 85.5 is

```
UPDATE STUDENT SET  Marks = 85.5
WHERE Name = 'Kanika';
```

(iv) (*a*) To delete data from a table the SQL command DELETE is used.

(v) (*d*)

```
INSERT INTO STUDENT VALUES (7,
'Rashmi', 'Humanities', 70.9, '12B');
```

PART 2

Subjective Questions

• Short Answer Type Questions

1. What is database? Give an example. What does DBMS stand for?

Ans. A collection of related information organised as tables is known as database e.g. INGRES, MySQL etc.

DBMS stands for DataBase Management System. It is a computer-based record keeping system.

2. What is the difference between 'Rows' and 'Columns' in a table?

Ans. In a table, rows are called records and columns are termed a fields. A row stores complete information of a record whereas column stores only similar data values for all records.

3. What is field in database? Give an example.

Ans. A field is an area, reserved for a specific piece of data. It is also known as attribute. e.g. Customer Name.

4. Define forms and what is the need of using them?

Ans. A form is a window or screen that contains numerous fields or spaces to enter data. Forms can be used to view and edit your data. It is an interface in user specified layout.

6. What does RDBMS stand for?

Ans. RDBMS stands for Relational Database Management System. It is a type of DBMS that stores data in the form of relations (tables).

6. How is data organized in a RDBMS?

Ans. A relational database is a type of database. It uses a structure that allows us to identify and access datain relation to another piece of data in the database. Data in a relational database is organized into tables.

7. Write the purpose of DBMS.

Ans. DBMS is used to store logically related information at a centralised location. It facilitates data sharing among all the applications requiring it.

8. Write any two uses of database management system.

Ans. The two uses of database management system are as follows

(i) DBMS is used to store data at a centralised location.
(ii) It is used to minimise data redundancy and data inconsistency.

9. Write any two advantages of using database.

Ans. The two advantages of using database are as follows

(i) It can ensure data security.
(ii) It reduces the data redundancy.

10. Give any two disadvantages of the database.

Ans. The two disadiantages of the database are as follows

(i) A database system creates additional complexity and requirements.
(ii) A database system is a multi-user software, which is less efficient.

11. A table named School (containing data of students of the whole school) is created, where each record consists of several fields including AdmissionNo (Admission Number), RollNo (Roll Number), Name. Which field out of these three should be set as the primary key and why?

Ans. AdmissionNo should be set as primary key because admission numbers are unique for each and every students of the school, which is not possible in the case with RollNo and Name.

12. Why Memo data type is preferred over Text data type for a field?

Ans. When the length of the field is more than 255 characters. Text data type is not capable to store the project description because its length cannot be more than 255 characters so, Memo data type is preferred over Text data type.

13. What happens when text is entered in a Number type field?

Ans. When we enter text in a Number field and press Enter or press Tab key, it displays a message that "The value you entered does not match the Number data type in this column."

14. List datatypes available in Numeric data type.

Ans. Datatypes available in numeric data type are TINYINT, SMALLCINT, MEDIUMINT, INT and BIGINT.

15. Write one example of data field for which you would set the Required property to Yes.

Ans. In a table, when we declare a field as a primary key, then the field's Required property must be set to yes because in a primary key field, we need to enter data always.

16. What is the purpose of Default Value field property?

Ans. If there is a situation when you want to enter same value for all records. Then, to avoid typing the same thing many times, you can set as a Default Value property.

17. Damini is a programmer in an institute and is asked to handle the records containing information of students. Suggest any 5 fields name and their data type of students database.

Ans.

Field Name	Data Type
RollNo	Number
Name	Text
Class	Text
Section	Text
Gender	Text

18. Create a table of Student based on the following table instance.

Column Name	Data Type	Length
ID	integer	
Name	varchar	15
Stream _Id	integer	

Ans. `CREATE TABLE STUDENT (ID Integer, Name varchar (15), Stream_Id Integer);`

19. Write a SQL command to create the table BANK whose structure is given below.

Table : BANK

Field Name	Datatype	Size	Constraint
ID_Number	integer	10	Primary key
Name	varchar	20	
B_date	date		
Address	varchar	50	

Ans. The SQL command to create a table as per given structure is as follows

```
Mysql> CREATE TABLE BANK (ID__Number
integer (10) PRIMARY KEY, Name varchar
(20), B__date Date, Address varchar
(50));
```

20. Insert some information into a table COLLEGE, whose structure is given below.

ROLL_NO	NAME	CLASS	BRANCH

Ans. (i) `Mysql>INSERT INTO COLLEGE (ROLL_NO, NAME, CLASS, BRANCH) VALUES (2, 'VIKAS',12, 'SCIENCE');`

(ii) `Mysql>INSERT INTO COLLEGE (ROLL_NO, NAME, CLASS, BRANCH) VALUES (3, 'RAJ', 10, 'SCIENCE');`

21. What is the value of Entry Required field?

Ans. The value of this property can be Yes or No. If entry required is Yes, the field cannot be absent i.e. should be necessarily present with a value.

22. What is table? Also, define Candidate Key.

Ans. A table consists of a number of rows and columns. Each record contains values for the attributes. A candidate key is the smallest subset of the super key for which there does not exist a proper subset that is super key. Any candidate key can be choosen to uniquely identify the records, it is called primary key.

23. What is Data Control Language?

Ans. Data Control Language is used to create roles, permissions, and referential integrity as well it is used to control access to the database by securing it. These SQL commands are used for providing security to database objects. These commands are GRANT and REVOKE.

24. What is Data Transaction Control Language?

Ans. Transaction control commands manage changes made by DML commands. These SQL commands are used for managing changes affecting the data. These commands are COMMIT, ROLLBACK, and SAVEPOINT.

• Long Answer Type Questions

25. Define Database Management System. Write two advantages of using database management system for school.

Ans. Database Management System (DBMS) is a collection of programs that enable users to create, maintain database and control all the access to the database. The primary goal of the DBMS is to provide an environment that is both convenient and efficient for user to retrieve and store information. The advantages of using DBMS for school are as follows

(i) In school, DBMS is used to store the data about students, teachers and any other related things at a centralised location.

(ii) It provides security to the personal information of the school, stored in it.

26. Distinguish between a record and a field in a table with an example.

Ans. Distinguish between a record and a field in a table are as follows

Record	Field
It is a collection of data items which represent a complete unit of information about a thing or a person.	It is an area with in the record reserved for a specific piece of data.
A record refers to a row in the table.	A field refers to a column in the table.
Record is also known as tuple.	Field is also known as attribute.
e.g. If Employee is a table, then entire information of an employee is called a record.	e.g. If Employee is a table, then empld, empName, department, Salary are the fields.

27. Write one example of each field, for which you would use

(i) Text data type (ii) Memo data type

Ans. (i) **Text data type** It allows to store text or combination of text and numbers as well as numbers that don't require calculations such as phone number. This data type allows maximum 255 characters to store. e.g. If Employee is a table and Emp_No, Name and Description are fields, then name will be a Text field. Because, Name is a character entry field.

(ii) **Memo data type** It allows long blocks of text that uses text formatting. e.g. In the Employee table, the field Description will be of Memo data type, because the length of description of employee may be large.

28. Define the following terms

(i) INSERT Command (ii) SELECT Command
(iii) DELETE Command (iv) DCL Command
(v) Template

Ans. (i) **INSERT Command** It is used to add a single record or multiple records into a table.

Syntax

```
INSERT INTO <table_name> (col1,
col2.....) VALUES (val1, val2);
```

(ii) **SELECT Command** It is used to query or retrieve data from a table in the database.

Syntax

```
SELECT column_list FROM table_name;
```

(iii) **DELETE Command** To discard unwanted data from a database, the delete command is used.

Syntax

```
DELETE FROM <table_name> WHERE
<condition>;
```

(iv) **DCL Command** DCL commands are used to assign security levels in database which involves multiple user setups. They are used to grant defined role and access privileges to the users.

(v) **Template** It is a complete tracking application with predefined tables, forms , reports, queries, macros and relationship.

29. Write SQL queries for the questions from (i) to (v) on the basis of table class.

No	Name	Stipend	Subject	AvgMark	Grade
01	Vikas	1200	Medical	67	B
02	Boby	1400	Humanities	78.4	B
03	Tarun	1000	Medical	64.8	C
04	Varun	1600	Non-medical	84	A
05	Atul	1800	Non-medical	92	A

(i) Select all the non-medical stream students from the class table.
(ii) List the names that have grade A sorted by stipend.
(iii) Arrange the records of class name wise.
(iv) List the records whose grade is B or C.
(v) Insert the new row with the following data. (06, 'Jack', 2800, 'Humanities', 98, 'A')

Ans. (i) `mysql> SELECT * FROM Class WHERE Subject= 'Non-medical';`

(ii) `mysql> SELECT Name FROM Class WHERE Grade='A' ORDER BY Stipend:`

(iii) `mysql> SELECT * FROM Class ORDER BY Name;`

(iv) `mysql> SELECT * FROM Class WHERE Grade IN ('B', 'C');`

(v) `mysql> INSERT INTO Class VALUES (06, 'Jack', 2800, 'Humanities', 98, 'A');`

30. Write SQL commands for the questions from (i) to (v) on the basis of table SHOP.

Table : SHOP

S_NO	P_Name	S_Name	Qty	Cost	City
S1	Biscuit	Priyagold	120	12.00	Delhi
S2	Bread	Britannia	200	25.00	Mumbai
S3	Chocolate	Cadbury	350	40.00	Mumbai
S4	Sauce	Kissan	400	45.00	Chennai

(i) Display all products whose quantity in between 100 and 400.

(ii) Display data for all products sorted by their quantity.

(iii) To list S_Name, P_Name, Cost for all the products whose quantity is less than 300.

(iv) To display S_NO, P_Name, S_Name, Qty in descending order of quantity from the SHOP table.

(v) Give S_Name for products whose name starts with 'B'.

Ans. (i) `mysql> SELECT * FROM SHOP WHERE Qty BETWEEN 100 and 400;`

(ii) `mysql> SELECT * FROM SHOP ORDER BY Qty;`

(iii) `mysql> SELECT S_Name, P_Name, Cost FROM SHOP WHERE Qty <300;`

(iv) `mysql> SELECT S_NO, P_Name, S_Name, Qty FROM SHOP ORDER BY Qty DESC;`

(v) `mysql> SELECT S_Name FROM SHOP WHERE P_Name LIKE 'B%';`

31. Write SQL commands for the questions from (i) to (v) on the basis of table MASTER (contains details of employees)

Table : MASTER

SNo	Name	Age	Department	Salary
1	Shyam	21	Computer	12000
2	Shiv	25	Maths	15000
3	Rakesh	31	Hindi	14000
4	Sharmila	32	History	20000
5	Dushyant	25	Software	30000

(i) Write a command to update the salary of the employee to 40000, whose SNo is 3.

(ii) Write a query to add a column Date_of_ Joining to the table MASTER.

(iii) Select Age, Department of those employees whose salary is greater than 12000.

(iv) List all data of table MASTER.

(v) Write a query to change the data type of a column Name to varchar with size 35.

Ans. (i) `mysql>UPDATE MASTER SET Salary= 40000 WHERE SNo =3;`

(ii) `mysql >ALTER TABLE MASTER ADD Date_of _ Joining date;`

(iii) `mysql>SELECT Age, Department FROM MASTER WHERE Salary>12000;`

(iv) `mysql>SELECT * FROM MASTER;`

(v) `mysql>ALTER TABLE MASTER MODIFY NAME VARCHAR (35);`

32. The director of a company uses a database to store data about job title. This is a part of the database given below.

Table : EmployeeSalary

Last Name	First Name	Dept	Payroll Number	Salary (₹)	JobTitle
Shen	James	Finance	A621	19500	Payroll Clerk
Gupta	Shruthi	Finance	M502	35000	Accountant
Bedi	Reeta	Human Resource	M421	18500	Secretary
Walker	Tia	Sales	W815	24000	Sales Represen-tative
Shafia	Ahmed	Factory	H219	39000	Factory Manager
Mittal	Chavi	Purchasin g	M134	20000	Purchasing Clerk

(i) How many records are there in this part of the database?

(ii) How many fields are there in this part of the database?

(iii) What is the job title of the employee with Payroll Number M421?

(iv) Which department has maximum employees and what are their Payroll Numbers?

Ans. (i) 6 (ii) 6 (iii) Secretary

(iv) Finance department and their Payroll Numbers are A621 and M502.

33. Consider the following database.

Product Code	Product Name	Dateof Sale	QtySold	Customer Name	Amount
P001	Pencil	05/10/11	5	Himanshu	25
P002	Eraser	04/01/12	4	Ali	8
P003	Sharpner	09/12/11	6	Deepak	12
P004	Whitener	25/04/11	2	Ankit	30
P005	Glue Pen	20/07/12	3	Ruchi	30

Answer the following questions.

(i) Write the name of the field that contains numeric data.

(ii) Identify the primary key field in the database.

(iii) Identify the field type of the DateofSale field.

(iv) Identify the names of the fields that contain textual data.

(v) The given table contains how many fields and records?

Ans. (i) QtySold and Amount

(ii) ProductCode

(iii) Date/Time data type

(iv) ProductCode, ProductName and CustomerName

Chapter Test

Multiple Choice Questions

1. Which of the following is not a data type?
(a) Picture/Graphic (b) Date/Time (c) Text (d) Number

2. The default data type for a field is
(a) number (b) auto number (c) currency (d) text

3. What is the use of Memo data type?
(a) To add table (b) To store objects created in other programs
(c) For long text entries (d) For short text entries

4. What data type should be chosen for a zipcode field in a table?
(a) Text (b) Number (c) Memo (d) All of these

5. You create a table in MS-Access. You decided to create two fields RollNo and Date_of_Birth, what will be the data type of Date_of_Birth column?
(a) Number (b) Text (c) Yes/No (d) Date/Time

Short Answer Type Questions

6. What do you mean by DDL?

7. How can you create table using CREATE command?

8. What is the use of forms?

9. What is RDBMS? How DBMS helps to avoid data inconsistency?

Long Answer Type Questions

10. Write the SQL commands for the questions from (i) to (v) on the basis of table Employee.

Table : Employee

Emp_no	E_name	Profile	Manager	Hire_date	Salary	Commission	Dept_no
8369	SMITH	CLERK	8902	1990-12-18	8000	NULL	20
8499	ANYA	SALESMAN	8698	1991-02-20	16000	300.00	30
8521	SETH	SALESMAN	8698	1991-02-22	12500	500.00	30
8566	MAHADEVAN	MANAGER	8839	1991-04-02	29850	NULL	20
8654	MOMIN	SALESMAN	8698	1991-09-28	12500	1400.00	30
8698	BINA	MANAGER	8839	1991-05-01	28500	NULL	30
8882	SHIVANSH	MANAGER	8839	1991-06-09	24500	NULL	10
8888	SCOTT	ANALYST	8566	1992-12-09	30000	NULL	20
8839	AMIR	PRESIDENT	NULL	1991-11-18	50000	NULL	10
8844	KULDEEP	SALESMAN	8698	1991-09-08	15000	0.00	30

(i) Display Employee Name and Salary of those employees whose salary is greater than or equal to 22000?
(ii) Display details of employees those are not getting commission.
(iii) Display employee name and salary of those employees who have their salary in range of 2000 to 4000?
(iv) Display the name, profile and salary of employee (s) who doesn't have manager?
(v) Display the name of employee whose name contains "A" as fourth alphabet.

11. Distinguish between Number and AutoNumber data type field. Give example of each.

Answers

Multiple Choice Questions

***1.** (a)* ***2.** (d)* ***3.** (c)* ***4.** (b)* ***5.** (d)*

For Detailed Solutions
Scan the code

CHAPTER 04

Web Applications and Security

In this Chapter...

- Working with Accessibility Options
- Networking Fundamentals
- Network Devices
- Network Topologies
- Internet
- Introduction to Instant Messaging
- Creating and Publishing Web Pages-Blog
- Using Offline Blog Editors
- Online Transaction and Online Shopping
- Internet Security
- Maintain Workplace Safety
- Prevent Accidents and Emergencies
- Protect Health and Safety at Work

A web application (web app) is an application program that is stored on a remote server and delivered over the Internet through a browser interface.

Common web applications include web mail, online retail sales and online auction, etc.

Security is fundamentally about protecting assets (data, hardware, reputation, etc.). Therefore, you should

- Identify potential threats
  Know how to react to an attack
- Detect and fix vulnerabilities

Working with Accessibility Options

Accessibility features are designed to help people with disabilities so that they use technology more easily. *For example*, a text-to-speech feature may read text out loud for people with limited vision, while a speech-recognition feature allows users with limited mobility to control the computer with their voice.

Launching Accessibility Options

To launch accessibility options, follow the given steps

***Step* 1** Click on **Start** button → **Control Panel**. Control Panel window will appear on your screen with various categories.

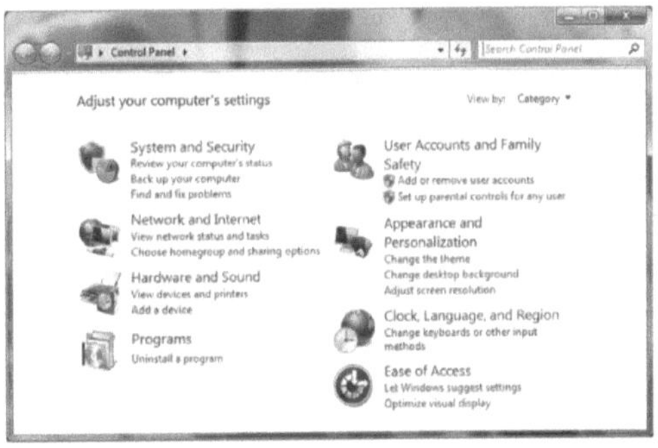

***Step* 2** Click on Ease of Access category. After this, Ease of Access window will appear.

***Step* 3** In the Ease of Access Center, click on Let Windows suggest settings.

***Step* 4** A window will provide in which you can change settings of keyboard, mouse etc.

***Step* 5** You can choose any options under Select all statements that apply to you.

Step 6 Click on Ease of Access Center. A window will appear.

Step 7 In this window, four options are given as

- **Start Magnifier** a display utility that makes the computer screen more readable by creating a separate window that displays a magnified portion of the screen.
- **Start Narrator** a text-to-speech utility that reads what is displayed on the screen–the contents of the active window.
- **Start On-Screen Keyboard** displays a virtual keyboard on the computer screen that allows people to type data by using a pointing device.
- **Set up High Contrast** a window showing settings for color and contrast of display.

Explore All Settings

Instead of looking for accessibility settings in various places on your computer, Windows bring all those settings together and organises them into categories that you can explore in Ease of Access Center. Some of them are

(i) Make the Computer Easier to See

If you occasionally have trouble seeing items on your screen, you can adjust the settings to make text and images on the screen appear larger, improve the contrast between items on the screen.

You can adjust many of these settings on the Make the computer easier to see page in the Ease of Access Center.

Open the Ease of Access Center, then select the options that you want to use.

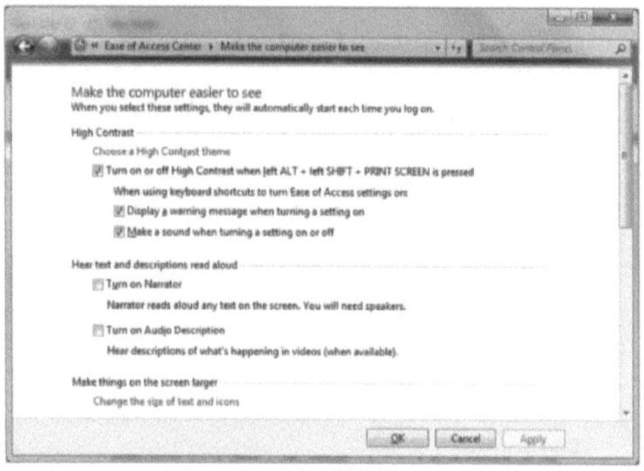

- **Choose High Contrast** This allows you to set a high-contrast color scheme that heightens the color contrast of some text and images on your computer screen.
- **Remove Background Images** This turns off all unimportant, overlapped content and backgroup images to help make the screen easier to use.

(ii) Make the Mouse Easier to Use

You can change how the mouse pointer looks and turn on other features that can help make it easier to use your mouse.

You can adjust these settings on the Make the mouse easier to use page in the Ease of Access Center.

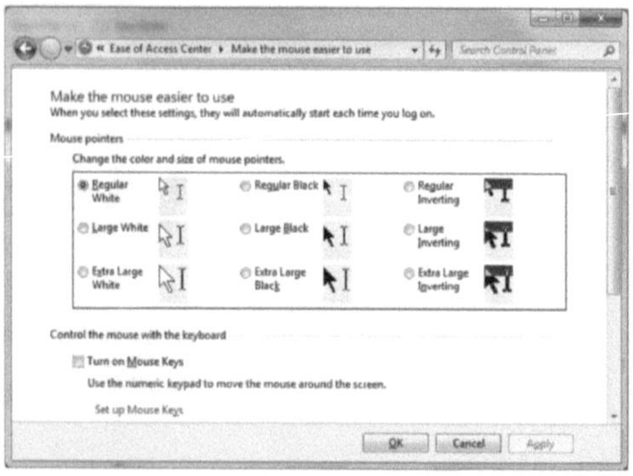

You can

- **Change the Color and Size of Mouse Pointer** You can use these options to make the mouse pointer larger or change the color to make it easier to see.
- **Turn on Mouse Keys** You can use this option to control the movement of the mouse pointer by using the numeric keypad.

(iii) Make the Keyboard Easier to Use

You can use your keyboard to control the mouse and make it easier to type certain key combinations. You can adjust these settings on the Make the keyboard easier to use page in the Ease of Access Center.

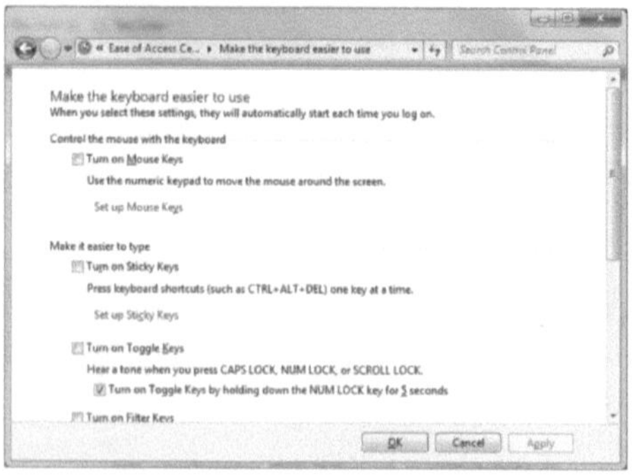

You can

- **Turn on Sticky Keys** This option sets Sticky Keys to run when you log on to windows. Instead of having to press three keys at once (Ctrl, Alt, Delete), you can use one key by turning on Sticky Keys and adjust settings.
- **Turn on Toggle Keys** This option sets Toggle Keys to run when you log on to windows. These keys can play an alert each time you press the Caps Lock, Num Lock or Scroll Lock Keys.

(iv) Use Text or Visual Alternatives to Sounds

Windows provide settings for using visual cues to replace sounds in many programs.

You can adjust these settings on the use text or visual alternatives for sounds page in the Ease of Access Center.

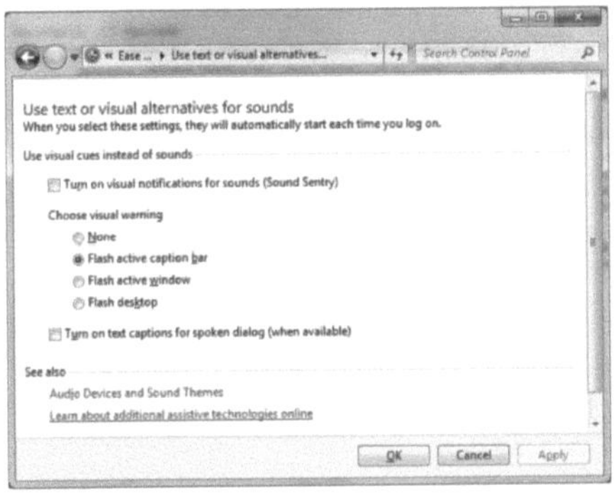

You can

- **Turn on Visual Notifications for Sounds** This option sets sound notifications to run when you log on the Windows. You can also choose how you want sound notifications to warn you.
- **Turn on Text Captions for Spoken Dialog** This option causes windows to display text captions in place of sounds to indicate that activity is happening on your computer.

Networking Fundamentals

A **network** can be defined as an interconnected collection of autonomous computers. A 'computer network' or simply a 'network' is a collection of computers and other hardware devices, interconnected by communication channels (satellites or cables) that allow sharing of resources and information. A computer networking is the practice for exchanging informations/services between two or more computer devices together for the purpose of sharing data. The speed of a network is measured in Mbps (Megabits per second).

Benefits of Networking

Computer network is very useful in modern environment, so some of the benefits of networking are discussed here :

- **File Sharing** Networking of computers helps the users to share data files.
- **Hardware Sharing** Users can share devices such as printers, scanners, CD-ROM drives, hard drives, etc.
- **Application Sharing** Applications can be shared over the network and this allows to implement client/server applications.
- **User Communication** This allows users to communicate using E-mail, newsgroups, video conferencing within the network.
- **Access to Remote Database** By networking, we are able to access to the remote database. It is easy for any person using his PC to make reservations for aeroplanes, trains, hotels, etc., anywhere in the world with instant confirmation within the network.

Types of Network

A network refers to a group of interconnected computers which are capable of sharing information and communication devices.

On the basis of coverage or geographical spread, a network can be divided into following types:

LAN (Local Area Network)

When a group of computers and its devices are connected in a small area, then this network is said to be a LAN. Computers or users in a local area network can share data, information, software and common hardware devices such as printer, modem, hard disk, etc. A LAN typically relies mostly on wired connections for increased speed and security but wireless connection also be a part of LAN. LAN are used within office building, school, etc.

MAN (Metropolitan Area Network)

This is basically bigger version of LAN and normally uses similar technology. It might cover few buildings in a city and might either be private or public. e.g. In a city, a MAN, which can support both data and voice might even be related to local cable television network.

WAN (Wide Area Network)

The network which connects the different countries network is known as WAN. It can be a group of LANs. The largest existing WAN is Internet. *For example,* a network of ATMs, BANKs, National Government Offices spread over a country or continents are examples of WANs.

Comparison between LAN, MAN and WAN

Basis	LAN	MAN	WAN
Speed	11 to 54 Mbps	11 to 100 + Mbps	10 to 384 Kbps, 1.83 to 7.2 Mbps
Range	Upto 5 km	5 km to 15 km	Upto 1000 km
Applications	Enterprise networks	Even replacement last mile access	Mobile phones, Cellular data

PAN (Personal Area Network)

PAN refers to a small network of communication. The range of a PAN is generally 10 metre. PAN may be wired using USB cables or wireless using wireless network technologies such as bluetooth, wireless USB, 2-wave and ZigBee. Bluetooth personal area network is also called a **piconet**. It can be composed of upto eight devices in a master–slave relationship.

Network Devices

Network devices are the components used to connect computer and other electronic devices together, so that they can share files or resources like printers or fax machines. The most common type of network devices used by the public to set-up a Local Area Network (LAN) are hub, switch, repeater and if online access is desired, a high-speed modem is required.

Some of them are described below

Hub

A hub is a device, which is used with computer systems to connect several computers together. It acts as a centralised connection to several computers with the central node or server. It is a multi-port device, which provides access to computers.

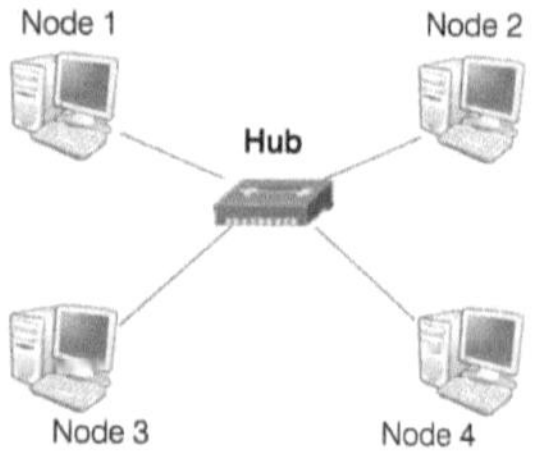

Switch

A switch is a hardware device, which is used to connect devices or segment of network with smaller subsets of LAN segments. The main purpose of segmenting is to prevent the traffic overloading in a network.

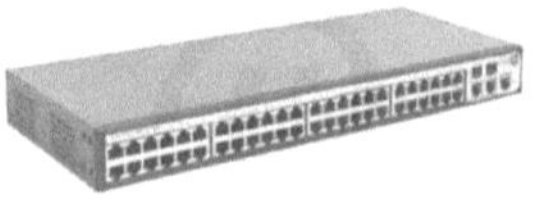

Switch

Repeater

Repeater is a hardware device, used to amplify the feeble signals, when they are transported over a long distance. When the signal is transmitted over a line, then due to resistance and other causes it accumulates noise. Due to this noise, the quality of signal degrades. The basic function of a repeater is to amplify the incoming signal and retransmit it to the other device.

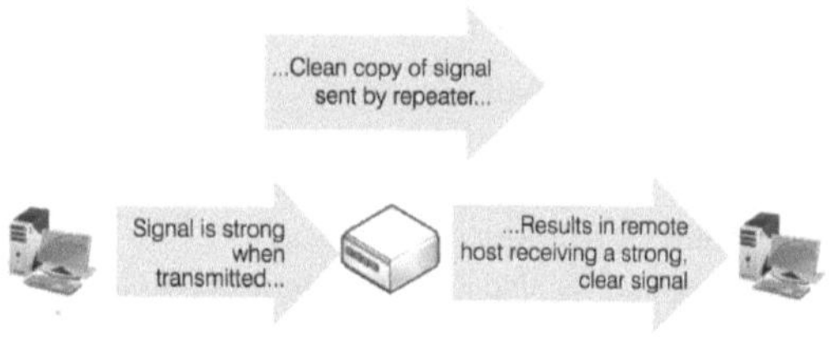

Repeater

Gateway

A gateway is a device which is used to connect dissimilar networks. The gateway establishes an intelligent connection between a local network and external networks, which are completely different in structure. Infact, the gateway is a node that routes the traffic from a workstation to outside network.

The gateway also acts as a proxy server and a firewall, which prevents the unauthorised access.

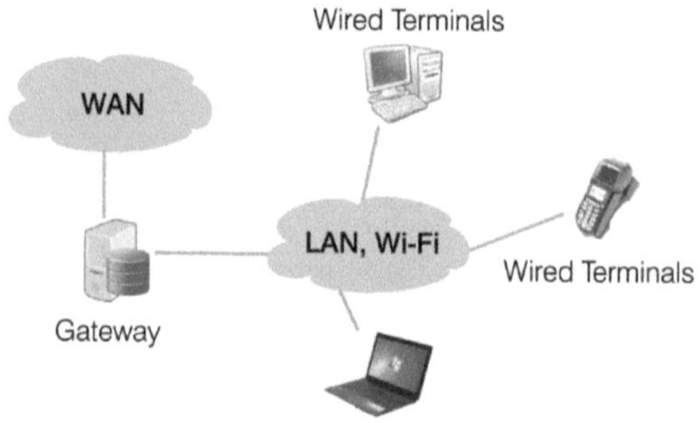

Bridge

Bridge serves a similar function as switches. A bridge filters data traffic at a network boundary. Bridge reduces the amount of traffic on a LAN by dividing it into two segments. Traditional bridge supports one network boundary, whereas switches usually offer four or more hardware ports. Switches are sometimes called **multi-part bridges**.

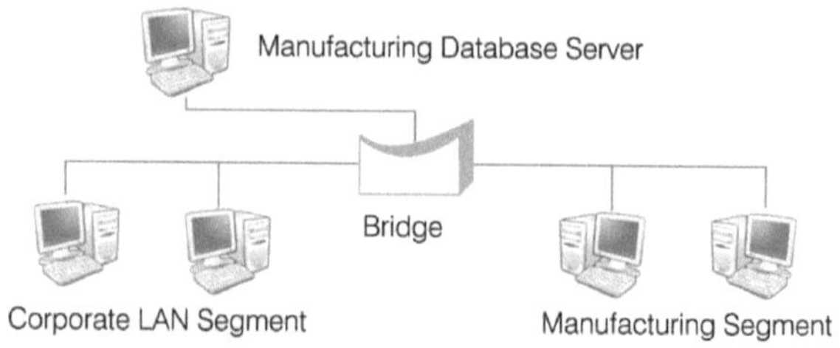

Bridge work with MAC addresses

Router

A hardware device designed to take incoming packets, analyse the packets, move the packets to another network, convert the packets to another network interface, drop the packets, direct packets to the appropriate locations, etc. A router functions similar to a bridge. However, unlike a bridge, a router passes data packets from one network to another network based on their IP addresses not MAC addresses.

Modem (Modulator/Demodulator)

Modem is a device that converts digital signal to analog signal (modulator) at the sender's site and converts back analog signal to digital signal (demodulator) at the receiver's end, in order to make communication possible *via* telephone lines.

NIC (Network Interface Card)

NIC provides the physical connection between the network and the computer workstation. With most LAN's cables, NIC is used for their connectivity.

Network Topologies

The network topology refers to the arrangement or pattern of computers, which are interconnected in a network. Commonly used network topologies are as follows

Bus Topology

It is a type of network in which the computers and the peripheral devices are connected to a common single length data line.

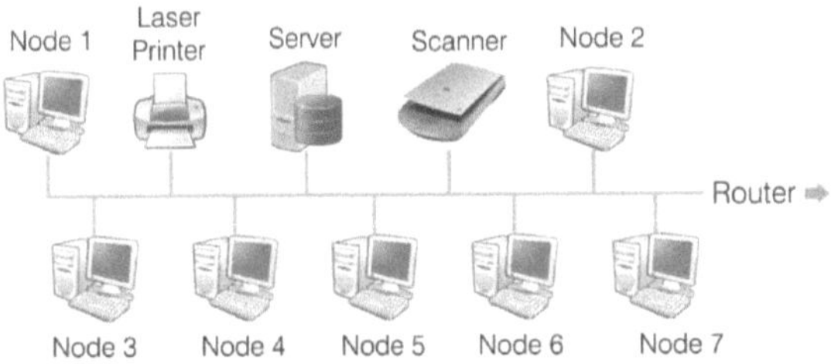

All the computers or devices are directly connected to the data line. The data is transmitted in small blocks, known as **packets**.

Ring or Circular Topology

In this type of topology, each node is connected to two and only two neighbouring nodes. The data travels in one direction only from one node to another node around the ring. After passing through each node, the data returns to the sending node.

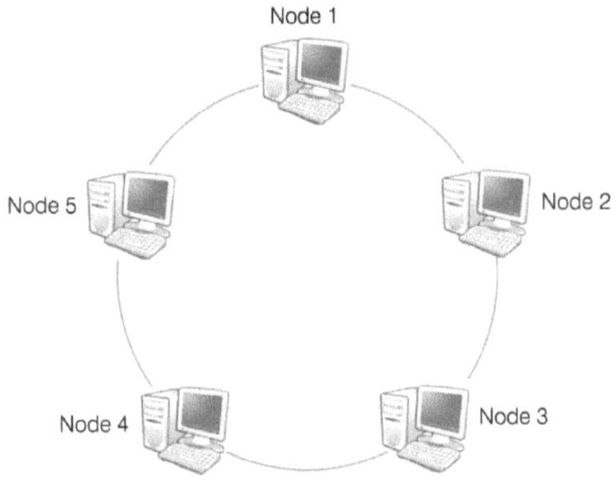

Star Topology

In this topology, there persists a central node called **server** or **hub**, which is connected to the nodes directly. If a node has to take information from other node, then the data is taken from that node through the central node or server.

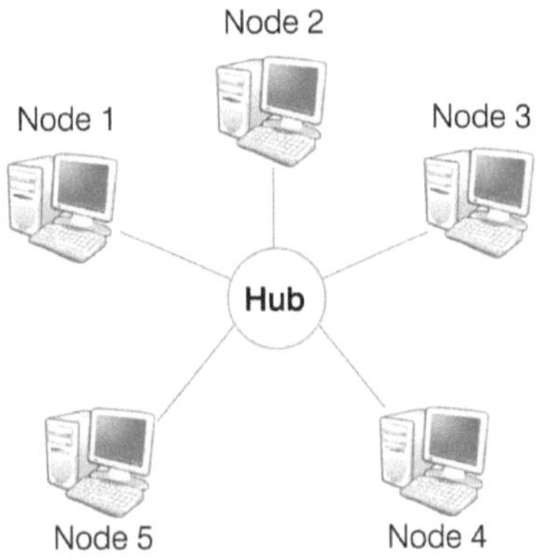

Mesh Topology

In this topology, each node is connected to more than one node, so that it provides alternative route, in case, if the host is either down or busy. It is also called a completely interconnected network. We can also call it as an extension to P2P network.

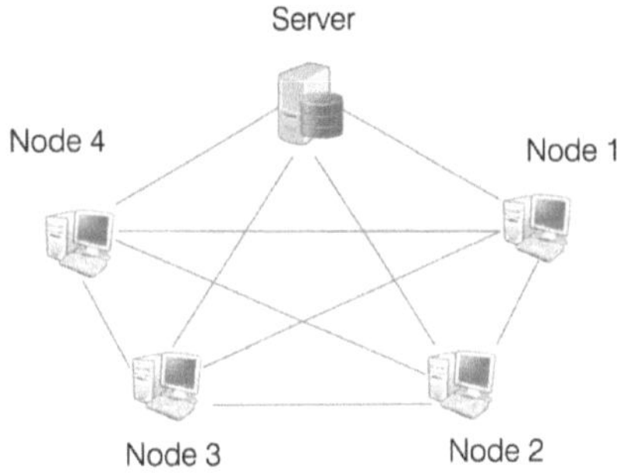

Tree Topology

It is an extension and variation of bus topology. Its basic structure is like an inverted tree, where the root acts as a server. In tree topology, the node is interlinked in the form of tree. If one node fails, then the node following that node gets detached from the main tree topology.

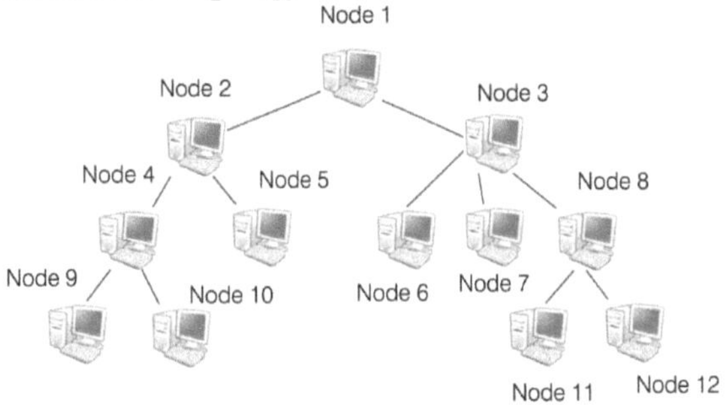

Models of Computer Networking

There are mainly two models of computer networking, which are as follows

(i) **Peer-to-Peer Network** It is also known as P2P network. This computer network relies on computing power at the edges of a connection rather than in the network itself. P2P network is used for sharing content like audio, video, data or anything in digital format. In P2P connection, a couple of computers is connected *via* a Universal Serial Bus (USB) to transfer files. In peer-to-peer networking, each or every computer may be worked as server or client.

(ii) **Client-Server Network** The model of interaction between two applications programs in which a program at one end (client) requests a service from a program at the other end (server). It is a network architecture which separates the client from the server. It is scalable architecture, where one computer works as server and others as client. Here, client acts as the active device and server behaves as passively.

Data Transfer on Network

Switching techniques are used for transmitting data across networks. Different types of switching techniques are employed to provide communication between two computers. These are

(i) **Circuit Switching** It is a methodology of implementing a telecommunication network in which two network nodes establish a dedicated communication channel (circuit), first through the network and then the message is transmitted through the channels. The main advantage of circuit switching is guaranteed delivery. The circuit switching guarantees the full bandwidth of the channels and remains connected for the duration of the communication session. The defining example of a circuit switched network is the early analog telephone network. When a call is made from one telephone to another, switches within the telephone exchanges create a continuous wire circuit between the two telephones for as long as the call last.

(ii) **Message Switching** It is a network switching technique, in which data is routed entirely from the source node to the destination node. In this technique, no physical path is established between source and destination in advance. During message routing, every intermediate switch in the network stores the whole message. If the entire network's resources are engaged or the network becomes blocked, the message switched network stores and delays the message until some resource become available for effective transmission of the message.

(iii) **Packet Switching** In packet-based networks, the message gets broken into small data packets. These packets are sent out from the computer and they travel around the network seeking out the most efficient route to travel as circuits become available. This does not necessarily mean that, they seek out the shortest route. The main advantage of packet switching is that the packets from many different sources can share a line, allowing for very efficient use of the communication medium.

Internet

The Internet has gained popularity and emerged as an important and efficient means of communication. The term Internet is derived from the words 'interconnection' and 'networks'. A network is a collection of two or more computers, which are connected together to share information and resources. The Internet is a world wide system of computer networks, i.e. network of networks. Through Internet, computers become able to exchange information with each other and find diverse perspective on issues from a global audience. Most of the people use Internet for sending and receiving E-mail and net surfing for retrieving information.

Network of networks

There are mainly three ways of connecting to the Internet, which are as follows

Dial-up Connection

It is a temporary connection, set-up between your computer and ISP server.

Dial-up connection uses the telephone line Public Switched Telephone Network (PSTN) and modem to connect to the Internet. The modem connects the computer through the standard phone lines, which serves as the data transfer medium. When a user initiates a dial-up connection, user needs to enter the password and specify a username and modem dials a phone number of an Internet Service Provider (ISP) to receive dial-up calls. DSL broadband service providers in India are BSNL, Airtel, Reliance, MTNL and Tata Indicom, etc. The ISP then establishes the connection, which usually takes about 10 s and is accompanied by several beeping and buzzing sounds.

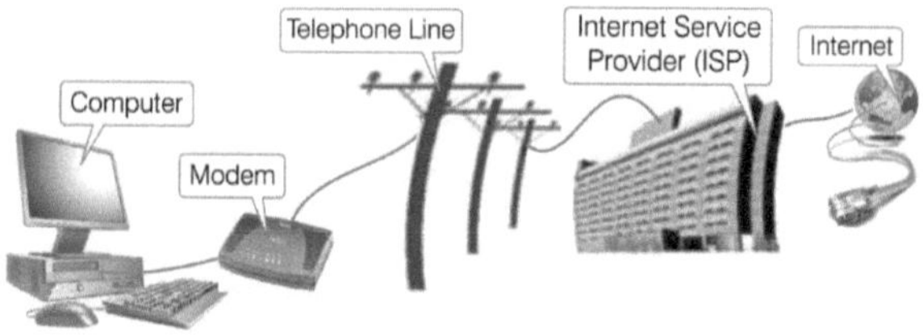

Dial-up connection

Broadband Connection

The term broadband commonly refers to high speed Internet access that is always ON and faster than the traditional dial-up access. It is the short form of broadband width, that uses a telephone line to connect to the Internet. Speed of broadband connection is measured in Mbps (Megabits per second). Broadband access allows users to connect to the Internet at greater speed than a standard 256 Kbps (Kilobits per second) modem or dial-up access. Broadband access requires the use of a broadband modem.

Broadband includes several high speed transmission technologies, which are as follows

(i) **Digital Subscriber Line** (DSL) It is a popular broadband connection which provides Internet access by transmitting digital data over the wires of a local telephone network. It uses the existing copper telephone lines for Internet access. A special modem is necessary in order to be able to use a DSL service over a standard phone line.
Faster forms of DSL, typically available to businesses are as follows
- High data rate Digital Subscriber Line (HDSL)
- Very High data rate Digital Subscriber Line (VHDSL or VDSL)
- Asymmetrical Digital Subscriber Line (ADSL)
- Symmetrical Digital Subscriber Line (SDSL)

(ii) **Cable Modem** This service enables cable operators to provide broadband using the same co-axial cables, that deliver pictures and sound to your TV set. A cable modem can be added to or integrated with a set-top box that provides your TV set for Internet access. They provide transmission speed of 1.5 Mbps or more.

(iii) **Broadband over Power Line** (BPL) It is the delivery of broadband over the existing low and medium voltage electric power distribution network. Its speed is generally comparable to DSL and cable modem speeds. BPL can be provided to homes using existing electrical connections and outlets. It is also known as power-band. BPL is good for those areas where there are no broadband connections, but power infrastructure exists. e.g. in rural areas.

Wireless Connection

Wireless broadband connects a home or business to the Internet using a radio link between the customer's location and the service provider's facility. Wireless broadband can be mobile or fixed. Unlike DSL and cable, wireless broadband requires neither a modem nor cables.

The distance between the devices connected to each other through a wireless Internet connection does not affect the rate of data transfer between them. Some ways to connect the Internet wirelessly are as follows

(i) **Wireless Fidelity** (Wi-Fi) It is a universal wireless networking technology that utilises radio frequencies to transfer data. Wi-Fi allows high speed Internet connections without the use of cables or wires. Wi-Fi networks can be designed for private access within a home or business. It can be used for public Internet access at 'hotspots' that offers Wi-Fi access such as restaurants, coffee shops, hotels, airports, convention centres and city parks.

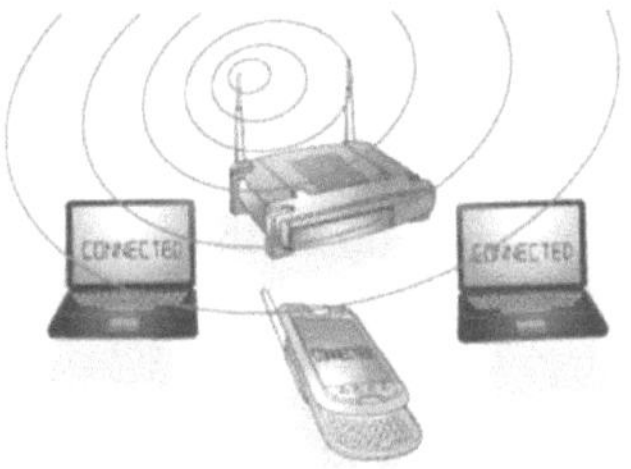

Wi-Fi network

(ii) **Worldwide Interoperability for Microwave Access** (WiMAX) Today, it is one of the hottest broadband wireless technology. These systems are expected to deliver Broadband Wireless Access (BWA) services upto 31 miles (45 km) for fixed stations and 3-10 miles (5-15 km) for mobile stations.
WiMAX would operate similar to Wi-Fi but at higher speed, over greater distances and for a greater number of users. It has the ability to provide services even in areas that are difficult for wired infrastructure to reach. Also, it has the ability to overcome the physical limitations of traditional wired infrastructure.

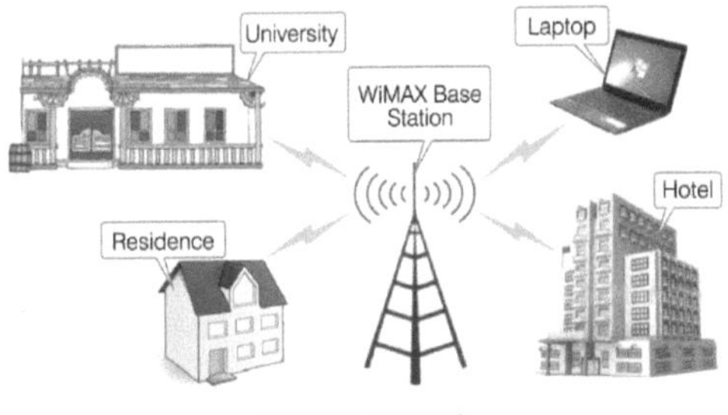

WiMAX network

Terms Related to Internet

Some terms related to Internet, which are as follows

World Wide Web (WWW)

It is a system of Internet servers that supports hypertext and multimedia to access several Internet protocols on a single interface. It is often abbreviated as the Web or WWW. It is a way of exchanging information between computers on the

Internet, trying to tie them together into a vast collection of interactive multimedia resources. It is only a portion of what makes up the Internet, but it is the fastest growing part of the Internet.

Web Page

The backbone of theWorld Wide Web is made up of files or documents called pages or web pages, that contain information and links to resources both **text** and **multimedia**. It is created using HTML (HyperText Markup Language).

Website

A group of related web pages that follow the same theme and are connected together with hyperlinks is called a Website. In other terms, "A website is a collection of digital documents, primarily HTML files, that are linked together and that exist on the web under the same domain." Each website is accessed by its own address known as **URL** (Uniform Resource Locator). e.g. http://www.carwale.com is a website, while http://www.carwale.com/new/ is a web page.

Two terms that are associated with a website are as follows

(i) **Home Page** The initial, main or first page of a website is known as home page. It can help the viewers to find out what they can find on particular site.

(ii) **Web Portal** It is a web page that combines useful information and links.

Web Browser

It is a software application that is used to locate, retrieve and display some content on the World Wide Web, including web pages. These are programs used to explore the Internet. It is an interface that helps a computer user to gain access over all the content on the Internet.We can install more than one web browsers on a single computer. The user can navigate files, folders and websites with the help of a browser. There are two types of web browsers, which are as follows

(i) **Text Web Browser** A web browser that displays only text-based information is known as text web browser. e.g. Lynx.

(ii) **Graphical Web Browser** A web browser that supports both text and graphic information is known as graphical web browser.

e.g. Internet Explorer, Firefox, Netscape, Safari (for Apple), Google Chrome, Opera, etc.

Web Server

It is a computer program that serves requested HTML pages or files from the web client.

A web client is the requesting program associated with the user. The web browser is a client that requests HTML files from web servers. Every web server that is connected to the Internet is associated with a unique address, i.e. IP address which is made up of a series of four numbers between 0 to 255 separated by periods. e.g. 68.178.157.132 or 68.122.35.127.

Web Address/URL

Web is a collection of documents (web pages) stored on computers around the world. Each web page has an address describing where it can be found. This address is known as web address or URL (Uniform Resource Locator). A web address identifies the location of a specific web page on the Internet, such as

http :// www. learnyoga.com

On the web, web addresses are called URLs. It is the web address for a website or a web page. The URL specifies the Internet address of a file stored on a host computer connected to the Internet.

Parts of URL

The URL contains three parts, which are as follows:

(i) The name of the protocol to be used to access the file resource.

(ii) A domain name that identifies a specific computer on the Internet.

(iii) A path name with hierarchical description that specifies the location of a file in that computer.

e.g.

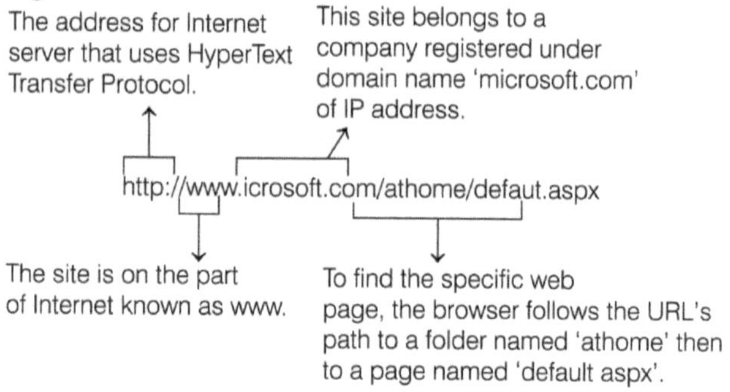

E-mail Address

E-mail stands for 'Electronic Mail'. It is a paperless method of sending messages, notes, pictures and even sound files from one place to another using the Internet as a medium. It is an individual name, which is used to send and receive E-mail on the Internet. It is used to specify the source or destination of an E-mail message.

e.g. arihant@gmail.com

Introduction to Instant Messaging

Instant Messaging (IM) is an Internet service that allows people to communicate with each other in real time through an instant messaging software. Unlike E-mail, instant messaging allows messages from one person to appear right away on the other person's computer screen right after the send button is pressed. Instant Messaging allows effective and efficient communication, allowing immediate receipt of acknowledgement or reply. However, IM is basically not necessarily supported by transaction control.

Many instant messaging services offer video calling features, Voice over Internet Protocol (VoIP) and web conferencing services. Web conferencing service can integrate both video calling and instant messaging abilities.

Instant Messaging Account

Messaging to each other participants need to be signed in to the same instant messaging software. To use instant messaging software, a user must have a valid instant messaging account. These accounts are differ in formats. Some IM software such as Yahoo! Messenger, Windows live messenger use E-mail addresses for managing the account and software such as Skype use standard names.

Instant Messaging Service

Here are services of instant messaging

- Accepts instant messages from external sites.
- Determines the user to which the message should be delivered and routers it accordingly.
- Accepts instant messages from internal hosts.
- Determines the destination system to which the message should be delivered and routes it accordingly.

Key Features of an Instant Messaging

Key features of an instant messaging are as follows

- Video calling
- Language translation (IM has an in-built translator).
- Going invisible (Your status can be shown as offline to your IM contact list).
- Encrypted messages (Text sent disappears from the receiver's phone automatically after they read it).
- In-built lock.
- Save messages for future reference.

Popular Instant Messaging Software

There are two kinds of instant messaging software, which are as follows

Application Based

This type of instant messaging software are downloaded from Internet and installed on user's computer. These are

- Whatsapp
- Viber
- Skype
- Facebook Messenger
- Google Talk
- WeChat

Web Based

This type of software is accessed using browsers such as google chrome etc. These are

- Meebo
- eBuddy
- MSN Web Messenger
- Yahoo! Web Messenger
- AIM Express
- MessengerFX

Google Talk Instant Messenger

Google Talk is also known as Gtalk, developed by Google. It is an instant messaging services that provides both text and voice communication developed by Google Inc. This is a free service from Google which requires users to have a google or gmail account to use the client.

Launching Google Talk

To launch Google Talk, follow the given steps

***Step* 1** Click on **Start** button.

***Step* 2** Click on **All Programs**. A sub menu will appear.

***Step* 3** Click on **Google Talk** and then click on Google Talk.

Or

***Step* 4** Double click on **Google Talk** icon which appear on desktop.

To Sign in, into your Google Talk Account

To sign in, into your Google Talk account, follow given step

***Step* 1** Use your Gmail account's username and password.

***Step* 2** Then click on **Sign in** button to sign into Google Talk.

Chatting on Instant Messenger

Chatting on Google Talk

Here are the steps to chat with a contact on Google Talk

***Step* 1** You can start chatting with your contact by double click on Google Talk. After this, a pop-up window will appear on the screen.

***Step* 2** Chat window has text box. In this box, you can type message and press **Enter** key.

***Step* 3** Message will sent to other person. He/She will read this message and reply your message if he/she wants.

To use Group Chat, just start a conversation with a contact, then click the drop–down on the right of the chat window and select Group Chat.

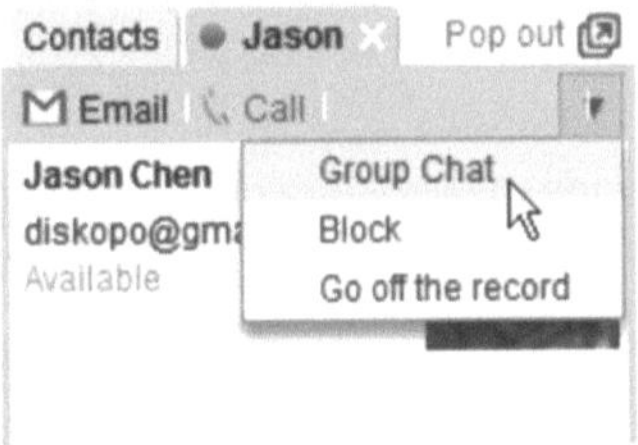

Chatting on G-mail

Besides sending and receiving E-mail, G-mail users have access to a range of additional features that can be quite useful. One of the most popular features of G-mail is chat.

Google Hangouts is Gmail's instant messaging feature, which allows you to talk in real time to friends and family.

To chat on G-mail, follow the given steps:

***Step* 1** Log in to your G-mail account with username and password.

***Step* 2** A window will appear on the screen.

***Step* 3** Left side of this window, contact list will be display.

***Step* 4** Double click on the contact name with which you want to start chat.

***Step* 5** After clicking on the contact name, a small pop-up window will be displayed on the right bottom side.

***Step* 6** Here, you can type the message for chatting.

Chatting on Yahoo

With Yahoo Messenger, you can chat and talk with your friends with yahoo accounts easily. You can use the Yahoo Messenger program on your computer or the app on your mobile device to call your friends and talk to them.

To chat on Yahoo, follow the given steps

***Step* 1** Open your **Yahoo account** with your Yahoo id and password.

***Step* 2** Click your Name or Yahoo id in the upper-left corner of the screen and select **Available** to show your contacts that you are online and able to chat.

***Step* 3** Click the **Minimized Yahoo Messenger** window at the bottom of the screen, if it automatically appeared when you went online.

***Step* 4** This maximizes window and displays any requests you received since the last time you were online. Click **Accept**, **Decline** or **Block** to act on an add request.

***Step* 5** **Click Compose Message → Instant Message**, to start a new conversation. Type a message and press Enter to send the message.

General rules and etiquettes to be followed while chatting

- The first thing you should check is, if the person infront of you is available or busy.
- It's simply rude to keep someone hanging, when they are expecting an answer from you. So, the polite thing would be to respond.
- Don't use offensive language.
- Avoid replying to negative comments with more negative comments.
- You may have to leave your seat for some reason but always inform the person infront that you are going to be away for sometime.

Creating and Publishing Web Pages – Blog

A blog is a website or a web page, in which an individual records opinion links to other sites on regular basis. A blog content is written frequently and added in a chronological order. It is written online and visible to everyone. A typical blog combines text, images and links to other blogs, web pages and other media related to its topic. In education, blogs can be used as instructional resources.

These blogs are referred to as **edublogs**. The entries of blog are also known as **posts**. A person who writes a blog or a weblog is known as **blogger**. Blogging is the act of posting content on a blog. There are some popular websites which offer blog service as follows

- Joomla
- Drupal
- Tumblr
- WordPress.com
- Blogger
- Weebly

Creating a Blog Account on WordPress

WordPress is a free personal publishing platform. It is an easy to use, fast and flexible blog script. It comes with a great set of features, designed to make your experience as a publisher as pleasant as possible. The steps to create a Blog account in WordPress are as follows

***Step* 1** Open a **web browser** e.g. Mozilla Firefox, Google Chrome etc., for creating a blog account.

***Step* 2** Type the URL www.wordpress.com in the address bar and press **Enter** key.

***Step* 3** Now, click on **Sign Up** button and after this, a page will appear as shown below

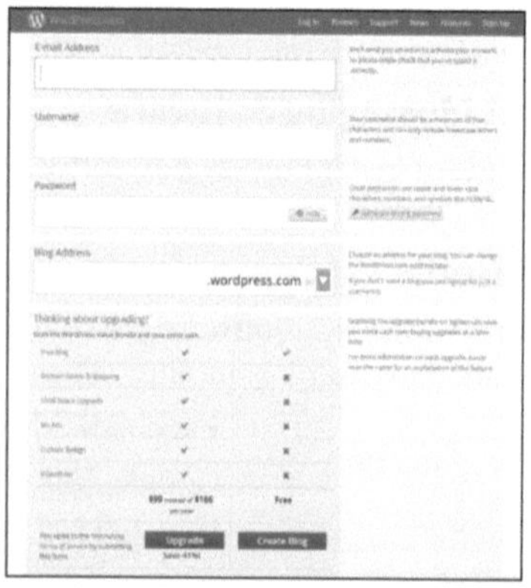

***Step* 4** Above page shows different fields such as E–mail Address, Username, Password etc.

- **E-mail Address** WordPress will sent an activation link to your e-mail id after clicking on Create Blog button. So, provide a valid e-mail address.
- **Username** This name will manage your blog.

- **Password** You must use strong password for securing purpose. You can use uppercase and lowercase letter with numbers and special symbols.
- **Blog Address** This address is used by viewer to view your blog.
- **Language** Here, you can choose language in which you want to write a blog.

Step 5 Click on **Create Blog** button.

Step 6 Now, you will get an activation link on your e-mail account. Open your e–mail and check to WordPress e-mail.

Step 7 Open that e–mail and click on **Confirm Now** link, your blog will be activated.

Step 8 After activating the blog, **WordPress Blog Account** will appear on your screen.

Adding Context to the Blog

Now, your blog is ready to use. To create a post, follow the given steps

Step 1 Click on **New Post** from the left side of the window. The following window will appear on the screen.

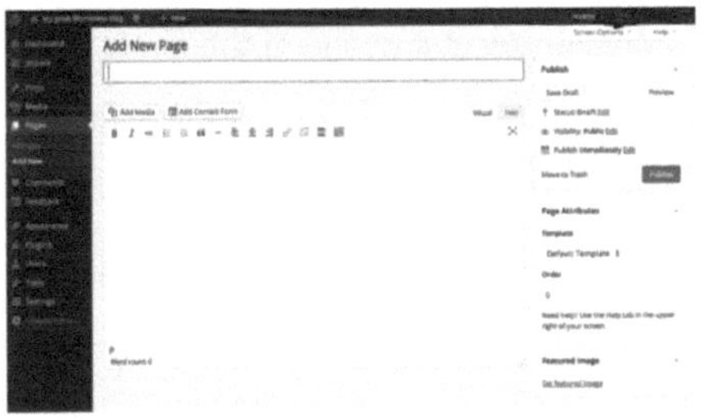

Step 2 Given the title to your blog in **Add New Page** text box. e.g. Arihant Publication.

Step 3 Type the content about Arihant Publication in content box and click on Publish button to publish your post.

Step 4 To view your post, open the web browser and type your blog address in the address bar.

Step 5 Now, you can see your post as well as others. Here, you can also comment on others post by clicking on **Leave a Reply** option.

Step 6 After typing the comment, click on **Post Comment** option.

Using Offline Blog Editors

An offline blog editor is a very useful tool for bloggers because it lets you create blog posts without an Internet connection. So, instead of waiting for an online editor to load, your can just work offline. Offline editors let you create, edit and format your content before you upload it to your website. Some popular free offline blog editors are

- Windows Live Writer (For Windows)
- BlogDesk (For Windows)
- Qumana (For Windows and Mac)
- MarsEdit (For Mac) free only 30 days trial

Online Transaction and Online Shopping

Online transaction is a payment method in which the transfer of fund or money happens online over electronic fund transfer. Online shopping is the process of buying goods and services from merchants over the Internet. Books, clothing, household appliances, toys, hardware, software and health insurance are just some of hundreds of products consumers can buy from an online store.

Benefits of Online Shopping

Some benefits of online shopping are as follows:

- Online shopping is very convenient. You can get products at home.
- Online shopping's websites provide millions of choices of product.
- They offer huge discount on goods and services.
- Online shops give us the opportunity to shop 24 × 7 hours and also reward us with cashback.
- Sending gifts to relatives and friends is easy by online shop.

Some Popular Online Websites

- **Amazon and Flipkart** An online shopping portal for buying consumer products.
- **Nykaa** An online shopping portal for beauty products.
- **IRCTC** An online portal for booking train tickets and seeing seat availability.
- **RedBus** An online portal for booking bus tickets.
- **Myntra** An online portal famous for branded clothing.

Transaction for Purchasing Goods at Flipkart

To purchase goods on Flipkart, follow the given steps:

Step 1 By web browser, open the **Flipkart** site.

Step 2 **Home page** of Flipkart will appear as shown below

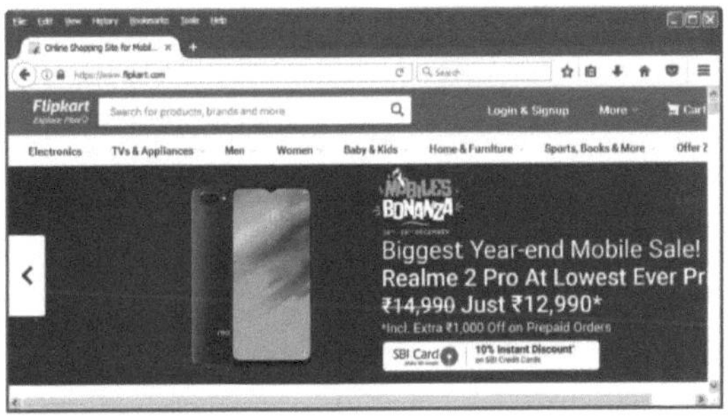

Step 3 Click on **Login** if you have an account on Flipkart otherwise click on Signup to register on Flipkart.

***Step* 4** A window will appear on screen with **Enter Mobile Number** field.

***Step* 5** Enter mobile number and click on **CONTINUE.** A window will be appear as shown below

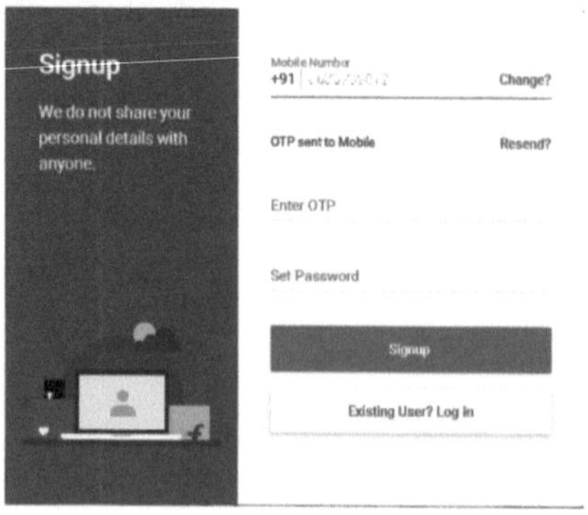

***Step* 6** You will received an **OTP** (One Time Password), enter this number and set password and then click on **Sign up.**

***Step* 7** Flipkart home screen will appear where different categories are given. You can select any category which you want.

***Step* 8** For example, select **Sports, Books** and **More.**

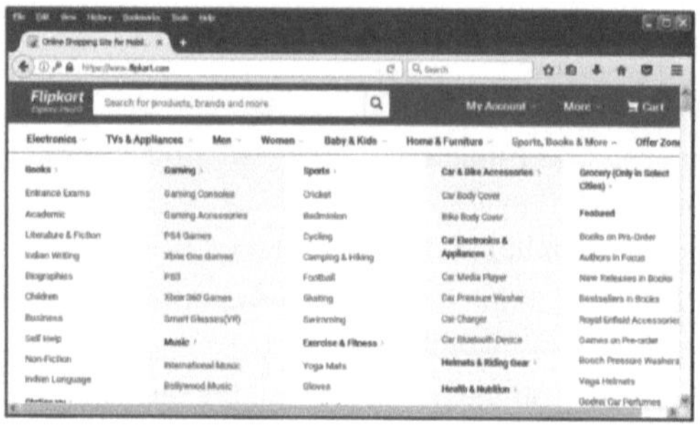

***Step* 9** The sub categories of Sports, Books and More will be display. In this category, select **Books → Indian Writing.**

***Step* 10** Click on the item which you want to purchase and then click on **Add to Cart.**

***Step* 11** Now, click on **My Cart** and Cart window will appear as shown below.

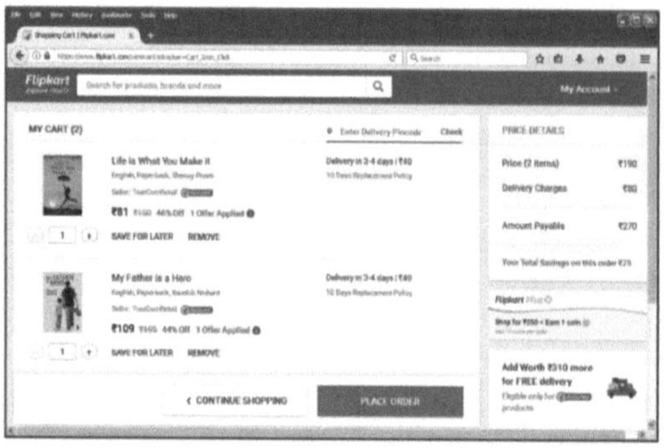

***Step* 12** Click on **Place Order.** A Delivery Address window will appear as shown below.

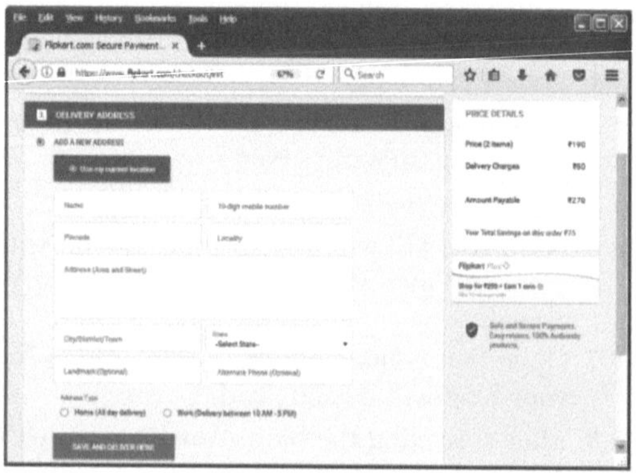

***Step* 13** Enter the details and click on **Save And Deliver Here.**

***Step* 14** The order summary page will appear and then click on **Continue** button.

***Step* 15** **Payment Options** window will appear as shown below. Here is the different payment methods. You can select any one of them. e.g. Cash on Delivery.

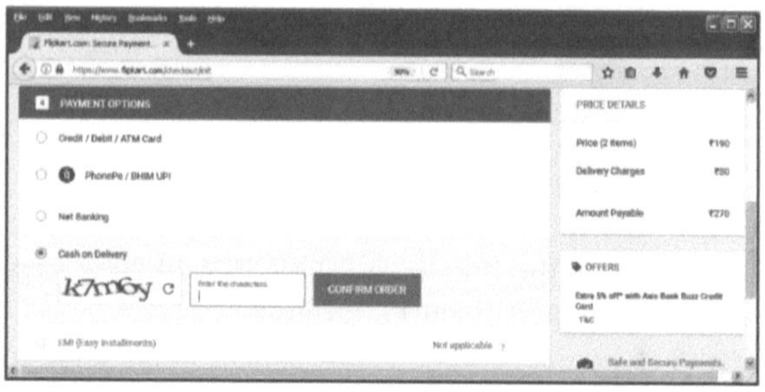

***Step* 16** Enter the characters in the given box and click on **Confirm Order.**

***Step* 17** After confirmation, a message will be received by you on registered mobile number.

Transaction for Booking Rail Tickets

An E–Ticket or electronic ticket is the digital ticket equivalent of a paper ticket. IRCTC (Indian Railway Catering and Tourism Corporation) is used to book and cancel rail tickets.

To book the ticket on IRCTC, follow the given steps

***Step* 1** Open the **IRCTC** site by www.irctc.co.in address. .

***Step* 2** Enter in **From** and **To** fields, class type and click on **Find Trains** option.

***Step* 3** Search the train and click on **Check Availability and Fare** to find the availability of train and book now.

***Step* 4** The following page will display. If you have an account on IRCTC then enter login name and password otherwise click on **REGISTER** button.

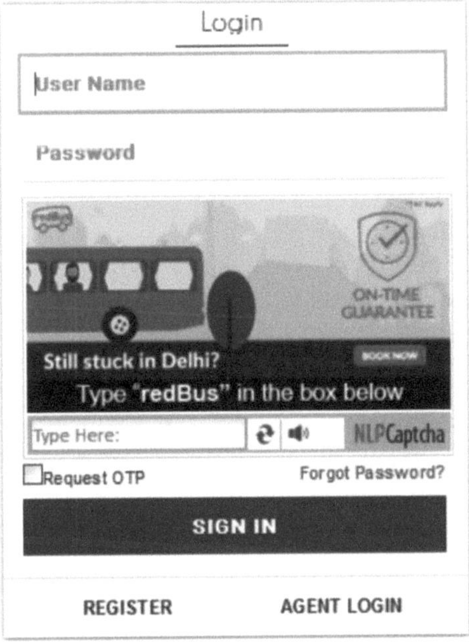

***Step* 5** Individual Registration page will appear, fill the details and click on **REGISTER** button.

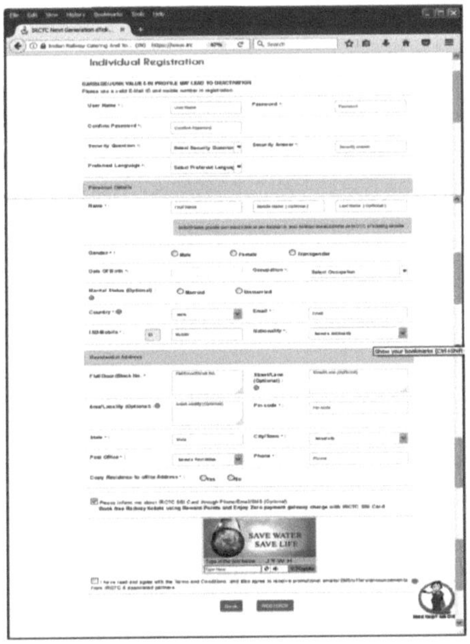

***Step* 6** After this, a window will appear as shown below

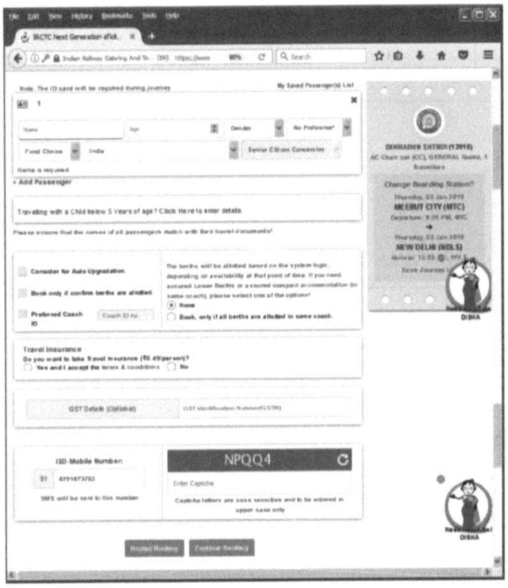

***Step* 7** Enter the required fields and click on **Continue Booking**.

***Step* 8** **Travelling Passengers** page will be appear as shown below.

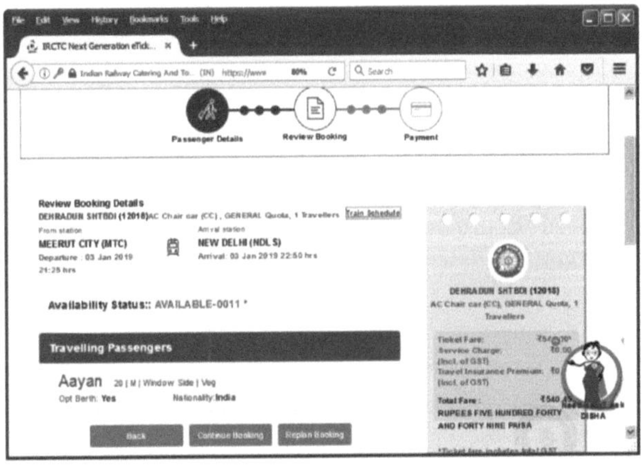

***Step* 9** Click on **Continue Booking**. Payment options page will be display on the screen. Select the appropriate option and enter details.

***Step* 10** **Payment Page** will be appear as shown below. Fill your bank details and click on **Proceed** button.

Step **11** E-ticket will be generated on screen as well as sent to your registered E-mail id.

Internet Security

It is a branch of computer security that deals specifically with Internet based threats. The Internet security prevents attacks targeted at browsers, networks, operating systems and other applications.

The main aim of Internet security is to set-up precise rules and regulations that can deflect attacks that arise from the Internet. Internet security relies on particular resources and criteria for safeguarding the data that is communicated or transferred online.

There are various best practices for Internet security, as follows

(i) **Use Secure Password** Your passwords are the most common way to prove your identity when using website, E-mail accounts and your computer itself. The use of strong password is therefore essential in order to protect your security and identity.

Do the following to choose the best password

- To create a strong password, simply choose three random words.
- You can use numbers, symbols and combination of uppercase and lowercase.
- Choose a password with atleast eight characters.
- Do not use your username, actual name or business name as password.
- Avoid to keep commonplace, dictionary word, your birthday date, etc.
- Avoid to use the word 'Password' and numerical sequence for password.

(ii) **Install Anti-Virus Protection** Only install an anti-virus program from a known and trusted source. Keep virus definitions, engines and software upto date to ensure your anti-virus program remains effective.

(iii) **Keep Software upto Date** Installing software updates for your operating system and programs in critical. Always install the latest security updates for your device.

- Turn on automatic updates for your operating system.
- Use web browser such as Google Chrome, etc., that receive frequent, automatic security updates.
- Make sure to keep browser plug-ins up to date.

(iv) **Always Keep your Firewall Active** Every computer is protected by a firewall. This firewall controls the flow of data over any network. Though firewall is the most secure feature in data protection. The firewalls provided mainly by the anti-virus developing companies are used.

(v) **Always use Secure Network Connection** Avoid doing crucial transaction over a public network. Any network other than your home or work network is an insecure network. Before using any connection other than trusted networks, always make sure that you secure the connection using appropriate VPN (Virtual Private Network) settings.

(vi) **Backup your Data** Backup on a regular basis, if you are a victim of a security incident, the only guaranteed way to repair your computer is to erase and re-install the system.

Various Cyber Threats

Phishing Phishing is an illegal practice in order to obtain personal and financial information, such as passwords, account IDs or credit card details and the attacker masquerading as a reputable personnel through the email or phone call. Phishing email messages are designed in such a way as to steal information. A person receives a message with a link, if the receiver clicks the link, the user is directed to a malicious website asking personal and financial details like credit card credentials, password, etc. If the user enter such personal and financial details, then that information will be taken away by the attacker and will be used for some illegal activities.

Spoofing Spoofing, as it pertains to cybersecurity, is when someone or something pretends to be something else in an attempt to gain our confidence, get access to our systems, steal data, steal money or spread malware.

E-mail Spoofing E-mail spoofing is the creation of fake emails that seem legitimate. E-mail spoofing is used in both fraudulent schemes and targeted attacks against organizations. Cybercriminals use this technique to convince victims that a message came from a trusted sender and nudge them into performing a specific action, such as clicking a phishing link, transferring money, downloading a malicious file, etc. For added credibility, attackers can copy the design and style of a particular sender's emails, stress the urgency of the task, and employ other social engineering techniques. SMTP (Simple Mail Transfer Protocol, the main email transmission protocol in TCP/IP networks) offers no protection against spoofing, so it is fairly easy to spoof the sender's address.

Spamming These mails are also called **junk mail** that arrives in the 'Spam' mail box of an email account. These mails include advertising pamphlets and brochures. These mails are sent indiscriminately to multiple mailing lists, individuals or newsgroups in order to advertise their products and services.

Cyberbullying Cyberbullying is a term referred to as bullying or harassing a person using electronic media like smart phones, tablets, computers through the use of communication tools like email, chatting session, text messages, posting rumors or embarrassing pictures on social media, etc. Due to the extensive use of internet, cyberbullying has become common, especially among teenagers.

Concept of Browser

A Web Browser is a software application that enables the users to access, retrieve and view the information and other resources on the Internet.

Some of the popular web browsers are Microsoft Internet Explorer, Microsoft Edge, Google Chrome, Mozilla Firefox, Opera and Netscape Navigator.

Types of Browsers

There are two types of browsers namely: graphical browsers and text-only browsers.

Graphical browser Most commercial browsers are graphical browsers within which audio, video and pictures can be run or viewed. All the browsers named earlier are graphical.

Text-only browser Lynx is an example of a text-only browser. It does not show up pictures, audio or video. In fact, it is meant for non-GUI systems. You may find it hard to believe but Lynx was once very popular.

Cookies

Cookies are small blocks of data created by a web server while a user is browsing a website and placed on the user's computer or other device by the user's web browser.

Backup

Backup is a copy of computer data taken and stored elsewhere, so that it may be used to restore the original after a data loss event. Before you make changes to critical data always make a duplicate. Even if you just made a backup yesterday-make another.

Anti-virus Software

Anti-virus software is a utility software program that are installed on your computer to protect it from viruses. Anti-virus is also known as **Anti-Malware** and it is a computer program used to prevent, detect and remove malware.Some of the popular antivirus software are

Norton, Kaspersky, McAfree, AVG, Bit defender, Avast, Quick Heal, etc.

To use an anti-virus first install it on the computer. After installation, you can use it to scan your whole system.

Scanning Folder/Files

You can also scan folders and files. Steps to scan folder/file are as follows

***Step* 1** Select the folder/file for scanning.

***Step* 2** Right-click on the selected folder. A drop-down menu appears.

***Step* 3** Click on the Scan for Viruses option. The scanning will start.

Clearing data in browser

To clear the data in browser(Google Chrome), follow the given steps

***Step* 1** Open the web browser window.

***Step* 2** Click on the button. A menu appears.

***Step* 3** Click on History option. A submenu appears.

***Step* 4** Again, click on History option. A window appears.

***Step* 5** Click on the Clear browsing data option. All the data browsed till date will get deleted.

Maintain Workplace Safety

Information Technology needs team work to succeed. The environment in an IT firm is that people sitting together and working on their terminals. While work is important, there are other issues of working among people, related to disparity of salaries, lack of work culture and many such aspects. Sometimes the working conditions are not safe and calamities happen. These topics are rarely looked at during university computer courses but have their own place in the lives of software people. In this chapter, we will learn about the different methods though which we can maintain a good health while at workplace.

Listed below are some cases in which physical pain can happen. They are as follows

- Fire
- Falls and slips
- Electrical mishandling or calamity
- Cuts in flesh

Signs used to designate for fall

Many of the topics brought up here are applicable to residential places of the people. We will stick to the office safety and health only here.

There are many possible causes for fire. Fire can be caused due to food being cooked, cigarettes being smoked, some garbage being burnt off, inadvertent flaring up of inflammable products, etc.

Some of the rules that companies have about fire safety are

- Do not smoke in the offices.
- Do not carry lighters or matches into the office.
- Do not use the elevator in times of fire in the building. Always use the staircase for such emergencies.
- Get trained in the use of fire extinguishers.

While the other rules are obvious, the rule no. (d), has many sub-parts to it. There are different kinds of fire extinguishers. Some are meant for electrical fires, while others for chemical fires. In case of chemical fires, you may throw water from the extinguishers and it will extinguish the fire.

A sign for no smoking

Occupational Safety and Health

It encompasses the social, mental and physical well-being of workers, that is the "whole" person.

Organizations can have become more effective, if they have safer and healthy workplaces. This is because:

- They have fewer days lost. Therefore, they have higher productivity.
- They can increase efficiency and quality. Because they have healthier workplace.

Electrical Safety

Employees should be trained in case of electrical fires and how to deal with such situations. In general, sand can be thrown into electrical fires. It should be known that water can never be used for electrical fires. Any other kind of fluid is also never used. There are many standards of wires and cabling that are conformant of fire safety and do not catch fire.

As the responsible person you must carry out and regularly review a fire risk assessment of the premises. This will identify what you need to do to prevent fire and keep people safe.

You may carry out the assessment in the following manner.

- Identify the fire hazards.
- Identify people at risk.
- Evacuate, remove or reduce the risks.
- Record your findings, prepare an emergency plan and provide training.
- Review and update the fire risk assessment regularly.

As part of the fire risk assessment plan, you will need to consider

- Emergency routes and exits
- Fire detection and warning systems
- Fire-fighting equipments
- The removal or safe storage of dangerous substances
- An emergency fire evacuation plan
- The need to consider vulnerable people, e.g. the elderly, young children or those with disabilities
- Staff fire safety training

A sign for flammable liquid

Fire Safety and Evacuation Plans

Some fire safety and evacuation plans are as follows

- A clear passageway to all escape routes.
- Clearly marked escape routes that are as short and direct as possible.
- Enough exits and routes for all people to escape.
- Emergency doors that open easily.
- A safe meeting point for staff.

A sign for fire exit

Fire Detection and Warning System

You must have a fire detection and warning system. You may need different types of detectors, depending on the type of building and the work carries out in it.

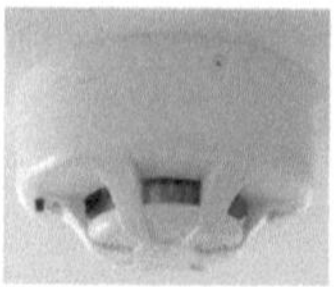
Smoke detector

Maintenance and Testing

You must carry out regular checks to make sure that:

- All fire alarms systems are working.
- The emergency lighting is working.
- You record any faults in systems and equipment.
- All escape routes are clear and the floor is in good condition.

- All fire escapes can be opened easily.
- Automatic fire doors close correctly.
- Fire exit signs are in the right place.

A sign for safe place

Fire safety is of the utmost importance in any building. As a business owner, you are responsible for ensuring that your workplace meets all required health and safety standards.

General Precautions in the Workplace

- Eliminate workplace hazards.
- Damaged electrical outlets, cords, cables, etc.
- Overloaded outlets and circuits.

Risk of electric shock sign

- Fire exit obstacles.
- Keep workspace and equipment clean, dry and well-ventilated and especially clean of oil and dust.

A sign for caution(Men at work)

Types of Fire

A		Ordinary Combustibles	Wood, Paper, Cloth, etc.
B		Flammable Liquids	Grease, Oil, Paint, Solvents etc.
C		Live Electrical Equipment	Electrical Panel, Motor, Wiring, etc.
D		Combustible Metal	Magnesium, Aluminum, etc.
K		Commercial Cooking Equipment	Cooking Oils, Animal Fats, Vegetable Oils etc.

Types of fires and its causing elements

Introduction to First Aid

At any moment, you or someone around you could experience an injury or illness. Using basic first aid, you may be able to stop a minor mishap from getting worse. In the case of a serious medical emergency, you may even save a life.

First aid sign

When you provide basic medical care to someone experiencing a sudden injury or illness, it is known as first aid.

Do not touch sign

In some cases, first aid consists of the initial support provided to someone in the middle of a medical emergency. This support might help them survive until professional help arrives.

In other cases, first aid consists of the care provided to someone with a minor injury. For example, first aid is often all that's needed to treat minor burns, cuts and insect stings.

First Aid Bandage

In many cases, you can use an adhesive bandage to cover minor cuts, scrapes or burns. To cover and protect larger wounds, you might need to apply a clean gauze pad or roller bandage.

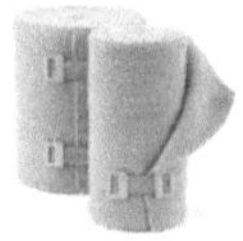

First aid bandage

First Aid for Burns

If you suspect that someone has a third-degree burn, call the hospital for ambulance. Seek professional medical care for any burns that:

- Cover a large area of skin
- Are located on the person's face, groin, buttocks, hands or feet.
- Have been caught by contact with chemicals or electricity.

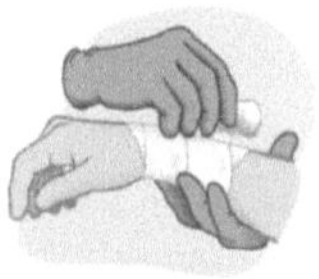

First aid for burns

To treat a minor burn, run cool water over the affected area for up to 15 min. If that's not possible, apply a cool compress to the area instead. Avoid applying ice to burned tissue, it can cause more damage.

Over-the-counter pain relievers can help relieve pain.

First Aid for Heat Stroke

When your body overheats, it can cause heat exhaustion. If left untreated, heat exhaustion can lead to heatstroke. This is a potentially life-threatening condition and medical emergency.

If someone is overheated, encourage them to rest in a cool location. Remove excess layers of clothing and try to cool their body down by doing the following:

- Cover them with a cool, damp sheet.
- Apply a cool, wet towel to the back of their neck.
- Sponge them with cool water.

Call the ambulance if they develop signs or symptoms of heatstroke, including any of the following:

- Nausea or vomiting
- Mental confusion
- Fainting
- Seizures
- A fever of 104 degree (40 degree C) or greater

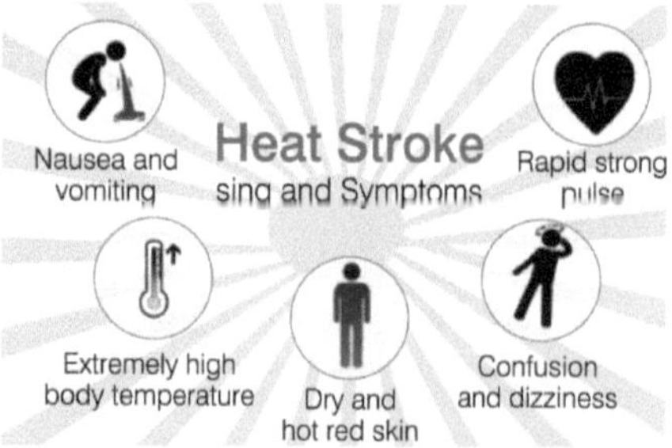

Heat stroke signs and symptoms

Prevent Accidents and Emergencies

An accident at workplace is a physical or mental injury following an incident or exposure.

If you accidentally get injured in the workplace, the injury is not necessarily caused by your work. *For example*, You are getting up from a chair and suddenly got a strain in your neck.

Workplace accident

How we examine an accident at work before we can assess if you have had an accident at work, we need the following

- Your employer's signature that the incident or exposure occurred as well as any additional information.
- Information about your employer's insurance company.
- A medical certificate describing the injury you have sustained due to the incident or exposure.

Types of Accidents in Workplace

There are many types of accidents that can occur in workplace. That's why it's so important for every small organisation to take the proper precautionary steps.

Some common accidents that can occur in workplace are as follows

(i) Slips, Trips and Falls

One of the common accidents in workplace is slipping on wet floor or you likely encountered slippery tiled surfaces.

Signs for slips, trips and falls

(ii) Muscle Strains

Another common type of accidents is strained muscles. This situation can occur with the person who lifts heavy weights at workplace.

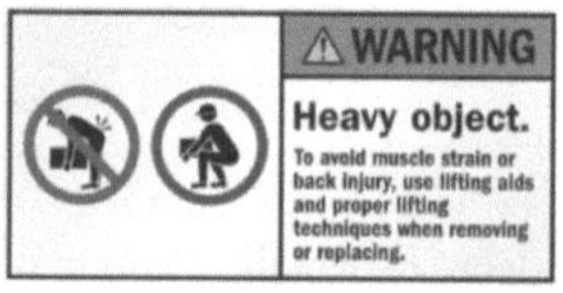

Muscle strain warning

(iii) Being Hit by Falling Objects

At the workplace, it may happen some objects may fall on you from shelves or out of the cupboard, causing some nasty injuries. Providing adequate storage cages and reminding employees of how to store items safely can go a long way to reducing this risk.

Falling object warning

(iv) Repetitive Strain Injury

RSI is another problem that's become increasingly commonplace at work over the years, though even now some employers don't seem to take it entirely seriously.

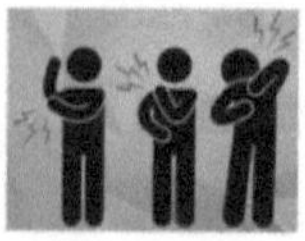

Repetitive strain injury

(v) Crashes and Collisions

Accidents resulting in crash or impact injuries are also quite frequent at work. Whether they involve cars, lorries or even smaller vehicles such as forklift trucks, they can have seriously nasty consequences.

To avoid crash warning sign to open the door nicely

(vi) Cuts and Lacerations

All sorts of office implements can end up leaving their user nursing a painful cut. From power saws to paper trimmers, it's easy to do yourself a mischief at work. The most common causes of these lacerations include poor training, inadequate safety procedures and failing to wear the proper protection.

Bosses can help prevent such accidents by providing adequate safety equipment and putting the right procedures (including training) in place.

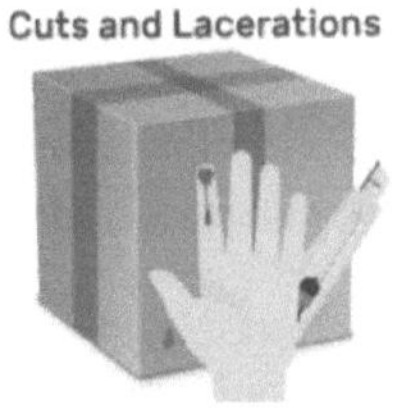

Cuts and lacerations at workplace

(vii) Inhaling Toxic Fumes

While most of us don't work with hazardous chemicals, those of us who do may be at risk of skin or eye reactions as well as potentially more serious injuries, when exposed to them without protection.

Protective equipment such as safety goggles is indispensable in these situations, so employers must be sure to provide workers with the gear they need to avoid dangerous exposure.

Hazardous substance warning

(viii) Exposure to Loud Noise

You might think that industrial deafness is a thing of the past and went out with all those old heavy industries, but that's not the case-not least because many industrial workers continue to be exposed to loud noises while at work.

Industrial deafness can also result in major compensation payouts further along the line, so it's very much in employers' interest to nip this particular problem in the bud. Safety measures such as ear protection can do much to prevent it.

High noise area warning

(ix) Walking into Objects

It's probably safe to say we have all done this at some point. Maybe you are chatting absent-mindedly or maybe you are feeling a little under the weather, when you suddenly find yourself on the sharp end of a door, table, wall or cabinet. Needless to say, these injuries can sting a bit.

Luckily, many such accidents can be avoided by reminding employees to be vigilant and putting unnecessary hazards out of the way where people won't walk into them.

(x) Fights at Work

These are not quite as rare as we might like to think. Simmering workplace tensions can bubble under for months or even years before spilling over into physical confrontation or alternatively one workmate can take another's opinion on last weekend's football the wrong way.

Fights in the workplace can, unsurprisingly, result in nasty injuries. Effective procedures for dealing with employee grievances can help reduce the risk of them coming to blows, though.

Handling Accidents

Good training, clear signage and access to the necessary safety equipment can all be a big help. Regular risk assessments are also a very good idea.

Your employer has a duty to protect you and tell you about health and safety issues that affect you. They must also report certain accidents and incidents, pay you sick pay and give you time off because of an accident at work should you need it.

On Hearing the Fire Alarm

- Close all the windows, doors and switch of non-essential services.
- Walk to the nearest assembly point.

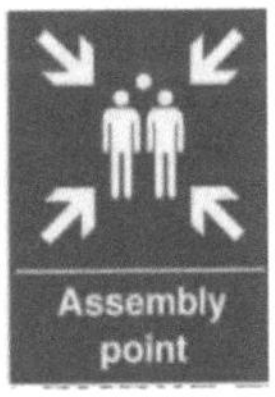

Sign for Assembly point

- Follow the emergency signs.
- Escape routes should be lit by emergency lighting so that people can use them safely, if an emergency occurs.

- Do not re-enter the building until permission is given by the person in charge of the evacuation.
- If the fire is small, but only if you are trained to do so use fire extinguishers to attempt to put the fire out.

Employees Must Know

- The nearest means of escape.
- The nearest fire alarm call point.
- The nearest fire appliance and how to use it (Only if trained to do so).
- Their assembly points.

In the Event of a fire

- Do not panic.
- Maintain silence.
- Do not use the lift.
- Do not attempt to push,pull, pass others.

Workplace Emergency

Nobody expects an emergency or disaster but the simple truth is that these can strike anyone, anytime and anywhere. You and your employees could be forced to evacuate your company, when you least expect it.

The best way to protect yourself, your workers and your business is to expect the unexpected and develop a well-thought out emergency action plan to guide you, when immediate action is necessary.

A workplace emergency is an unforeseen situation that threatens your employees, customers or the public; disrupts or shuts down the workplace operations; or causes physical or environmental damage.

Emergency Action Plan

An emergency action plan covers designated actions employers and employees must take to ensure employee safety from fire and other emergencies. Putting together a comprehensive emergency action plan that deals with all types of issues specific to your worksite is not difficult.

You may find it beneficial to include your management team and employees in the process.

Developing an Evacuation Plan

A disorganised evacuation plan can result in confusion, injury and property damage. i.e. why when developing your emergency action plan it is important to determine the following

- Conditions under which an evacuation would be necessary.
- A clear chain of command and designation of the person in your business authorised to order an evacuation or shutdown. You may want to designate an "evacuation warden" to assist others in an evacuation and to account for personnel.
- Specific evacuation procedures, including routes and exits. Post these procedures, where they are easily accessible to all employees.

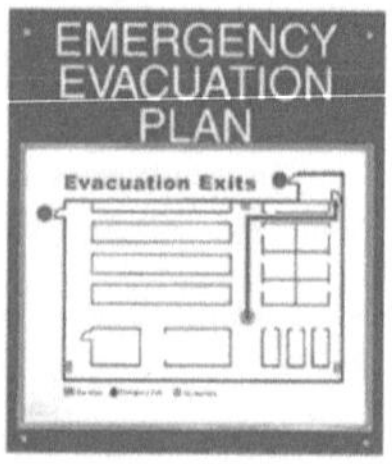

Emergency evacuation plan

- Procedures for assisting people with disabilities or who do not speak English. Special attention must be given to evacuation procedures for persons with disabilities.
- Designation of what, if any, employees will continue or shut down critical operations during an evacuation. These people must be capable of recognising, when to abandon the operation and evacuate themselves.
- A system for accounting for personnel following an evacuation. Consider employees' transportation needs for community-wide evacuations.

Establishing Evacuation Routes and Exits

When preparing your emergency action plan, designate primary and secondary evacuation routes and exits. To the extent possible under the conditions, ensure that evacuation routes and emergency exits meet the following conditions:

- Clearly marked and well lit.
- Wide enough to accommodate the number of evacuating personnel.
- Unobstructed and clear of debris at all times.
- Unlikely to expose evacuating personnel to additional hazards.

Conducting Fire Exit Drills and Evacuations

To ensure that building occupants are prepared for an emergency evacuation, fire drills must be conducted periodically. A safe and orderly evacuation is more important than a quick evacuation.

Fire exit drills are only conducted by or under the direction of the Fire Safety Specialist for the Environmental Health, Safety and Risk Management office.

Emergency Procedure Maps

Emergency procedures diagrams are located within buildings throughout each campus. These diagrams provide floor plans showing the locations of emergency exits and emergency equipment (such as fire extinguishers) and maps for evacuation routes and emergency assembly areas.

Protect Health and Safety at Work

Hazards

A hazard is any source of potential damage, harm or adverse health effects of the people at workplace. Hazard is a potential source of harm to the health of the worker or employee.

But, the exact meaning of the word hazard can be confusing, as often it is combined with the term risk.

Examples of a Hazard

Workplace hazards can come from a wide range of sources. General examples include any substance, material, process, practice, etc. that has the ability to cause harm or adverse health effect to a person or property.

Workplace Hazard	Example of Hazard	Example of Harm Caused
Thing	Knife, Blade	Cut
Substance	Benzene	Leukaemia
Source of Energy	Electricity	Shock, electrocution
Condition	Wet floor	Slips, falls
Process	Welding	Metal fume fever
Behaviour	Bullying	Anxiety, fear, depression

Types of Hazards

Let us specify the types of hazards are as follows:

- Biological hazards
- Chemical hazards
- Ergonomic hazards
- Physical hazards
- Psychosocial hazards
- Safety hazards

Identification of hazards

General Evacuation Procedure during hazard

By identifying hazards at your workplace, you will be better prepared to control or eliminate them and prevent accidents, injuries, property damage and downtime.Firstly, a key step in any safety protocol is to conduct a thorough hazard assessment of all work environments and equipments.

The following points must be kept in mind:

1. First aid boxes at various places in the office.
2. Trained first aiders-on all floors of a building.
3. Knowledge of the nearest casualty department or local hospital.
4. Access to call for an ambulance.
5. Ability to provide immediate assistance to casualties with illnesses or injuries caused by a specific hazard at work.

Health and Safety at Work

Your employer has to carry out a risk assessment and do what's needed to take care of the health and safety of employees and visitors. This includes deciding how many first aiders are needed and what kind of first aid equipment and facilities should be provided.

Healthy Living

You should maintain a healthy lifestyle to survive and sustain in the workplace.

The various factors that should be taken into account to maintain a healthy living are as follows

- Watch your plate
- Watch your waist and weight
- Watch your steps
- Watch your stress level
- Watch your change
- Watch your tobacco and alcohol consumption

Chapter Practice

PART 1
Objective Questions

• Multiple Choice Questions

1. Which of the following is an application program that is stored on a remote server and delivered over the Internet?
(a) Web application
(b) System application
(c) Internet application
(d) None of the above

Ans. (*a*) A web application is an application software that runs on a web server. Web applications are accessed by the user through a web browser with an active network connection.

2. Computer connected with LAN
(a) work fast
(b) go online
(c) can E-mail
(d) can share information or peripheral devices

Ans. (*d*) Computer connected with LAN can share information or peripheral devices. Peripheral devices can be scanner, printer, etc.

3. A group of computers connected together with the help of cables within an office building is called
(a) PAN (b) WAN (c) MAN (d) LAN

Ans. (*d*) Using LAN, we can connect computers within a building only. A Local Area Network is the one which connects computers and devices in a limited geographical area such as home, school, office or any closely placed group of buildings. It provides very high speed.

4. Network formed between computers which exists across the continents is called
(a) LAN (b) WAN (c) MAN (d) WLAN

Ans. (*b*) Across the continents, computers can be connected using WAN only. A Wide Area Network is one which covers a broad area.

5. Digital information is converted into analog information by the modem at
(a) destination computer
(b) source computer
(c) Both (a) and (b)
(d) Neither (a) nor (b)

Ans. (*b*) Digital information is converted into analog information by the modem at source computer. A modem is a device that converts digital signals to analog signals, so that signals can travel over telephone lines. This device also converts analog signals to digital.

6. Modulation and demodulation are performed by
(a) microwave (b) satellite
(c) modem (d) fibre optic

Ans. (*c*) Modulation and demodulation are performed by modem. The full form of modem is Modulator-Demodulator.

7. A modem is connected between a telephone line and a
(a) computer (b) serial port
(c) network (d) communication adapter

Ans. (*a*) Modem is a device that enables computers and other equipments to communicate with each other using telephone lines.

8. Which of the following is not a transmission medium?
(a) Telephone lines (b) Co-axial cable
(c) Modem (d) Microwave

Ans. (*c*) Telephone lines, co-axial cable and microwave are transmission medium but modem is a network device that converts analog signal to digital signal and *vice-versa*.

9. What can you do with the Internet?
(a) Exchange information with friends and colleagues
(b) Access pictures, sounds, video clips and other media elements
(c) Find diverse perspective on issues from a global audience
(d) Internet exchange information, access pictures,find diverse perspective on issue from a global audience

Ans. (*d*) Internet is a collection of interconnected computer networks. It uses the standard Internet Protocol suite (TCP/IP) to serve the billions of users worldwide. In other words, it is a network of networks that exchange information, access pictures, find diverse perspective on issue from a global audience.

10. The first network was
(a) ARPANET (b) Internet
(c) NSFnet (d) NET

Ans. (*a*) The Advanced Research Projects Agency NETwork (ARPANET) was the world's first operational packet switching network .

11. Which of these services will not be provided by a typical Internet Service Provider (ISP)?
(a) An E-mail address
(b) Modem
(c) A connection to the Internet
(d) Technical help

Ans. (*a*) ISP refers to a company that provides Internet services, modem, connection and technical help but it does not provide an E-mail address.

12. To join the Internet, the computer has to be connected to a
(a) Internet architecture board
(b) Internet society
(c) Internet Service Provider
(d) None of the above

Ans. (*c*) Internet Service Provider is used to join the Internet. An Internet Service Provider (ISP) is an organisation which provides you with access to the Internet *via* wired or wireless connection.

13. Wireless broadband can be
(a) mobile
(b) fixed
(c) Both (a) and (b)
(d) None of the above

Ans. (*c*) Wireless broadband can be mobile or fixed. It does not require modem or cable.

14. Nick connects to the Internet at home using a laptop computer with a wireless connection. Nick is going to change use desktop computer using a 1 Gbps ethernet cable connection.
Which of these should be the result of making the changes?
(a) Increased portability and decreased speed
(b) Decreased portability and increased speed
(c) Increased portability and increased speed
(d) Decreased portability and decreased speed

Ans. (*b*) If Nick is going to change to a desktop computer using a 1 Gbps ethernet cable connection, then it decreased portability and increased speed.

15. .... is a collection of web pages linked together in a random order.
(a) A website (b) A web server
(c) A search engine (d) A web browser

Ans. (*a*) A website is a collection of web pages linked together in a random order and displays related information on a specific topic.

16. Home page helps viewers to find out what they can find on the particular site? Home page is the
(a) first page of a website
(b) index page
(c) about page
(d) None of the above

Ans. (*a*) Home page refers to the initial or main or first web page of a website, sometimes called the front page. It can help the viewers to find out what they can find on particular site.

17. Which client software is used to request and display web pages?
(a) Web server (b) Multimedia
(c) FTP (d) Web browser

Ans. (*d*) A web browser is a program that your computer runs to communicate with web servers on the Internet, which enables you to download and display the web pages that you request.

18. .... is an example of text-based browser which provides access to the Internet in the text-only mode.
(a) Mozilla Firefox (b) Lynx
(c) Internet Explorer (d) All of these

Ans. (*b*) Lynx is a highly configurable text-based web browser.

19. In URL, http://www.arihant.com/index.htm, which component identifies the website?
(a) http (b) www.arihant.com
(c) /index.htm (d) All of these

Ans. (*b*) www.arihant.com, because domain name identifies the website.

20. In URL, http://www.arihant.com/index.htm, which component identifies the path of a web page?
(a) http
(b) www.arihant.com
(c) /index.htm
(d) All of the above

Ans. (*c*) /index.htm, because path name identifies the path of a web page.

21. Manoj has to set-up a network between his devices at home which included a smart phone, a laptop and a personal computer. What type of network he would be setting up for the same?
(a) PAN (b) MAN
(c) WAN (d) None of these

Ans. (*a*) Manoj would be setting up a PAN (Personal Area Network) which is best suited for set-up involving a computer, a cell phone and/or a handheld computing device such as a PDA.

22. Anila works in a Multi National Company (MNC) and needs to work online from home also. She requires fast Internet connection. Which type of Internet connection in your view would be best suited for her?

(a) Dialup (b) Broadband
(c) Both are suitable (d) None of these

Ans. (*b*) Anila should prefer broadband connection. Broadband connections are much faster than a Dial-up connection because these signals carry more data. The speed of a broadband connection is measured in Mbps (Megabits per second).

23. Sharvan Joshi is a student of Political Science and is a keen researcher of political issues related to various countries and states. He wants to share his research and his own opinions on these issues on day-to-day basis with everyone on World Wide Web (WWW). He is also interested in collecting views of others to enhance his research and knowledge related to his area of interest. He belongs to a middle class family and cannot afford his own website. Also being a non- technical person, he cannot create a dynamic website to deal with day-to-day inputs. Suggest an easy way for Sharvan to achieve the same.

(a) He should develop an E-mail id
(b) He should develop his research online
(c) He should develop a blog
(d) He should use instant messaging app

Ans. (*c*) Sharvan should develop a blog. Blogs are used to create personal web pages by non-technical and technical users. Users can easily share their comments, thoughts and convey messages about events, news, etc.

24. What type of hazard are caused by stress violence at workplace?

(a) Chemical hazard (b) Safety hazard
(c) Psychological hazard (d) None of these

Ans. (*c*) Psychological hazard can be caused by unwanted stress of work completion on time, quarrelling, violence or fights with colleagues, lack of control and respect, etc. at workplace.

25. Which type of hazard can cause skin irritation, illness or breathing problems?

(a) Chemical hazard
(b) Biological hazard
(c) Slipping hazard
(d) None of the above

Ans. (*a*) Chemical hazard depends on the physical, chemical and toxic properties of the chemical in any form (solid, liquid or gaseous). This type of hazards can cause skin irritation, illness or breathing problems.

26. Do not use the elevator in times of fire in the building. Always use............... for such emergencies.

(a) office space (b) washroom
(c) staircase (d) None of these

Ans. (*c*) One should use staircase in times, of fire in the building. He/She must not use elevator during that time, as the electricity can go off and the person might stuck in the elevator. Neither one should use washroom or any other office at the time of emergency.

27. If you have a safer and healthy workplace, there will be fewer days lost and will have higher

(a) Employee satisfaction
(b) Productivity
(c) Stress levels
(d) None of the above

Ans. (*b*) A safer and healthier workplace can increase the productivity of the employee. Occupational safety encompasses the social, mental and physical well-being of workers, i.e. the "whole" person. Organisations can become more effective if they have safer and healthy workplaces.

28. You should conduct regular fire drills in order to

(a) Eliminate workplace hazards
(b) Prepare for emergencies
(c) Carry out the risk assessment
(d) None of the above

Ans. (*a*) The organisation should regular fire drills in order to check whether the fire extinguishers are working properly, to train the staff and to give complete knowledge of the evacuation gates. These are important to eliminate workplace hazards.

29. Which of the following falls in the category of workplace emergency?

(a) Earthquake (b) Tornadoes
(c) Both (a) and (b) (d) None of these

Ans. (*c*) A workplace emergency is an unforeseen situation that threatens your employees, customers, or the public; disrupts or shuts down the workplace operations; or causes physical or environmental damage. Both earthquake and tornadoes falls in the category of workplace emergency.

30. What is the full form of RSI?

(a) Repetitive Strain Injury
(b) Rational Strain Injury
(c) Repetitive Stress Injury
(d) Risk Strain Injury

Ans. (*a*) RSI stands for Repetitive Strain Injury. RSI is another problem that's become increasingly common place at work over the years, though even now some employers don't seem to take it entirely seriously.

• Case Based MCQs

Direction *Read the case and answer the following questions.*

31. A WAN spans a large physical distance. The Internet is the largest WAN, spanning the Earth. A WAN is a geographically-dispersed collection of LANs. A network device called a router connects LANs to a WAN. In IP networking, the router maintains both a LAN address and a WAN address. They are owned by multiple organisations.

(i) What is the full form of WAN?
(a) World Area Network
(b) Wide Area Nest
(c) Wide Area Network
(d) Wide Access Network

(ii) How much physical distance a WAN spans to?
(a) Large distance
(b) Small distance
(c) Within the same building
(d) Within the office/home

(iii) ……….. is the largest WAN, spanning the Earth.
(a) Technology (b) Internet
(c) Distance (d) Router

(iv) A ……….. connects LANs to a WAN.
(a) Wire (b) Pen drive
(c) CD (d) Router

(v) How many organisation(s) own WAN?
(a) Single organisation (b) Multiple organisations
(c) Two organisations (d) None of these

Ans. (i) (*c*) WAN stands for Wide Area Network. It is a type of network. It covers a broad area.

(ii) (*a*) A WAN covers a large physical distance. It consists of one or more LANs.

(iii) (*b*) Internet is the largest WAN, spanning the Earth. Internet is widely used by students, teachers, educational institutes, engineers, scientists and others to research, to gather the information and do many more things. Internet is the largest encyclopaedia for all age groups. It is also becoming a major source of entertainment for general public.

(iv) (*d*) A router connects LANs to WAN. A router is attached to one or more networks to forward packets from one network to another.

(v) (*b*) WAN is owned by multiple organisations. A WAN is used by government organisations and businesses.

32. World Wide Web (WWW) or simply web is a set of programs, standards and protocols that allows the multimedia and hypertext files to be created, displayed and linked on the Internet. The World Wide Web was invented in 1989. It became publicly available on Internet for the first time. The Internet is the physical network of computers all over the world. The World Wide Web is a virtual network of websites connected by hyperlinks (or "links"). Websites are stored on servers on the internet, so the World Wide Web is a part of the Internet.

(i) WWW stands for ……….. .
(a) World Wide Web (b) Word Wide Web
(c) World Way Web (d) Web World Wide

(ii) World Wide Web (WWW) is a set of programs, standards and protocols that allows the multimedia and hypertext files to be created, displayed and linked on the ……….. .
(a) ARPNET (b) CSNET
(c) Internet (d) CERN

(iii) Which of the following is/are stored on servers of Internet?
(a) WWW (b) Websites
(c) Internet (d) Links

(iv) ARPANET stands for ……….. .
(a) Advanced Research Projects Agency NETwork
(b) Advanced Research Product Agency NETwork
(c) Advanced Research Process Agency NETwork
(d) Advanced Research Plan Agency NETwork

(v) In which year was WWW invented?
(a) 1988 (b) 1989 (c) 1990 (d) 1992

Ans. (i) (*a*) WWW stands for World Wide Web. The World Wide Web, commonly known as the Web, is an information system, where documents and other web resources are identified by Uniform Resource Locators (URL), which may be interlinked by hyperlinks and are accessible over the Internet.

(ii) (*c*) World Wide Web (WWW) is a set of programs, standards and protocols that allows the multimedia and hypertext files to be created, displayed and linked on the Internet.

(iii) (*b*) Websites are stored on servers of Internet. Websites are the building block of www.

(iv) (*a*) ARPANET stands for Advanced Research Projects Agency NETwork.ARPANET was the first wide-area packet-switched network with distributed control and one of the first networks to implement the TCP/IP protocol suite.

(v) (*b*) Sir Tim Berners-Lee invented the World Wide Web in the year 1989.

PART 2

Subjective Questions

• Short Answer Type Questions

1. Name the term defined by given below statement: "A group of computers connected to each other by a link."

Ans. Computer network is defined as a group of computers connected to each other by a link that allows sharing of resources and information.

2. What is the definition of networking? **[CBSE Textbook]**

Ans. A computer networking is the practice for exchanging information/services between two or more computers together for the purpose of sharing data.

3. What are the main types of computer networks?

Ans. Following are the three main types of computer networks, based upon the geographical area as follows:

(i) Local Area Network (LAN)
(ii) Metropolitan Area Network (MAN)
(iii) Wide Area Network (WAN)

4. What is the main purpose of switch?

Ans. A switch is a hardware device which is used to connect devices or segment of network with smaller subsets of LAN segments.

5. Identify the following devices.

(i) A device that is used to connect different types of networks. It performs the necessary translation, so that the connected networks can communicate properly.

(ii) A device that converts data from digital bit stream into an analog signal and *vice-versa*.

Ans. (i) Router (ii) Modem

6. What is the advantage of mesh topology?

Ans. In mesh topology, each node is connected to more than one node, so that it provides alternative route. In case, if the host is either down or busy.

7. Give the names of models of computer networking.

Ans. There are mainly two models of computer networking as follows:

(i) Peer-to-Peer network (ii) Client-server network

8. How many techniques are used for transmitting data across network?

Ans. There are three techniques used for transmitting data across network : circuit switching, packet switching and message switching.

9. Write two advantages of using Internet.

Ans. Advantages of using Internet are as follows:

(i) It is used for communication, entertainment, searching information and for providing many types of services.
(ii) It provides the facility of E-mail.

10. Name any five DSL broadband service providers in India.

Ans. BSNL, Airtel, Reliance, MTNL and Tata Indicom are the five DSL broadband service providers in India.

11. Write the name of any two Internet Service Provider (ISP) in India.

Ans. MTNL and Airtel are the two Internet Service Provider (ISP) in India.

12. Name any two ways of wireless connections of Internet. Ramya wants to connect all the computers of her office wirelessly in order to avoid uncoordinated cables. Which wireless technology would be best suitable for her office?

Ans. Wi-Fi and WiMax are the two ways of wireless connections of Internet. Wi-Fi technology would be best suitable for her office to avoid cabling. Because, it allows high speed Internet connections without the use of cables or wires.

13. Write the full form of following terms.

(i) WiMAX
(ii) BPL

Ans. (i) **WiMAX** Worldwide Interoperability for Microwave Access.

(ii) **BPL** Broadband over Power Line

14. What can a user do with WWW? Name any two major services provided by Internet.

Ans. Using WWW (World Wide Web), a user can download files, listen to music, view video files and jump to other documents or websites by using hypertext links. E-mail and WWW are the two major services provided by Internet.

15. Mr. Lal owns a factory which manufactures automobile spare parts. Suggest him the advantages of having a web page for his factory.

Ans. The web page provides the information to the clients about his factory of spare parts. Moreover, he can receive the order on the Internet from the clients using the web page.

16. Name two web browsers of Internet.

Ans. Internet Explorer and Google Chrome are the two web browsers of Internet.

17. What is URL? Can we use URL to access a web page? How?

Ans. URL means Uniform Resource Locator. It is a unique address of a web page on the Internet. It specifies the Internet address of a file stored on a host computer connected to the Internet. Yes, as a location on a web server, which is called a website and each website has a unique address known as URL. So, an URL can be used to access a web page.

18. Identify web addresses and E-mail addresses from the following.

(i) www.scrapbook.com
(ii) aba@scrapbook.com
(iii) www.countrywide.co.in
(iv) 123@hotshot.co.in

Ans. Key features of an Instant Messaging are:

(i) and (iii) are web addresses.
(ii) and (iv) are E-mail addresses.

19. Write any two key features of an Instant Messaging (IM).

Ans. Key features of an Instant Messaging are :

(i) Video calling
(ii) Language translation

20. List any five application based instant messaging software. **[CBSE Textbook]**

Ans. Whatsapp, Viber, Skype, WeChat, Google Talk

21. Who is blogger? List any five websites that provide blog service.

Ans. A person who writes a blog or a weblog is known as blogger. Blogging is the act of posting content on a blog.

Any five websites that provide blog service listed below

(i) Joomla (ii) Blogger
(iii) Word Press.com (iv) Tumblr
(v) Drupal

22. Explain the purpose of a blog.

Ans. The main purpose of blog is to convey messages about events, announcements, need, review, etc. Blogs are usually managed using a web browser and this requires active internet connection.

23. Laluma Chakradhar wants a broadband connection to access her mails and stay informed about the latest happening in the field of Biotechnology. Can you suggest two Internet Service Providers (ISPs) of India to be approached for the same?

Ans. BSNL and Airtel

24. Explain the concept 'Watch Your waist and weight; to maintain a healthy body at workplace'.

Ans. The explanation of the concept 'Watch Your waist and weight; to maintain a healthy body at workplace' is

(i) Encourage the use of weighing scales, measuring tapes and devices to monitor individual physical fitness.
(ii) Place weighing scales, measurement tapes and body mass index charts in strategic locations.

25. What are the advantages of having safer and healthy workplace?

Ans. The advantages of having safer and healthy workplaces are as follows:

(i) They have fewer days lost, therefore they have higher productivity.
(ii) They can increase efficiency and quality, because they have healthier workplace.

26. What are physical hazards?

Ans. Physical hazards can be any factors within the environment that can harm the body without necessarily touching it. It can be caused by radiation (microwave, radio wave), pressure extremes (high pressure or vacuum), constant loud noise, high exposure to sunlight/ultraviolet rays,temperature extremes (hot and cold), etc.

27. What are slipping and tripping hazards?

Ans. Slipping hazards are causes through spills or trips such as cords running across the floor or water spilled on the floor. Tripping hazards are caused through falls such as working from heights, including ladders, scaffolds, roofs, etc.

28. How does water and foam fire extinguisher work?

Ans. Water and foam fire extinguishers extinguish the fire by taking the heat element away from the fire. Water extinguishers are for class A fires. Class A fires involve ordinary combustile materials, such as cloth, wood, paper, rubber and many plastics.

29. How does carbon dioxide fire extinguisher work?

Ans. Carbon Dioxide fire extinguishers extinguish fire by taking away the oxygen element of the fire triangle and also be removing the heat with a very cold discharge. Carbon dioxide can be used on Class B and C fires. They are usually ineffective on Class A fires.

30. How does wet chemical fire extinguisher work?

Ans. Wet chemical is a new agent that extinguishes the fire by removing the heat of the fire triangle and prevents re-ignition by creating a barrier between the oxygen and fuel elements.

Wet chemical of Class K extinguishers were developed for modem, high efficiency deep fat fryers in commercial cooking operations. Some may also be used on Class. A fires in commercial kitchens.

31. Write down any three points of differences between LAN, MAN and WAN.

Ans. Three major points of differences among LAN, MAN and WAN are as follows

(i) **In terms of geographical area** WAN covers the area across the continents, MAN covers area within a city while LAN covers area within a building.

(ii) **In terms of distance** The approximate distance covered by WAN is unlimited, of MAN is upto 160 km while that of LAN is upto 5 km.

(iii) **In terms of speed** The speed with which the data travels in case of WAN is 10 to 38.4 Kbps, 183 to 7.2 Mbps, while that of MAN is 11 to 100 Mbps and of LAN is 11 to 54 Mbps.

32. Explain the LAN and WAN.

Ans. A **Local Area Network (LAN)** is a computer network covering a small geographical area like a home, office or small group of buildings such as buildings in a school. Computers connected to a LAN can share information and peripheral equipments.

A **Wide Area Network (WAN)** is used to connect LANs and other types of network together, so that users and computers in one location can communicate with users and computers in other locations.

33. What is the use of repeater in a network?

Ans. In a network, repeater receives a weak signal coming from a source and amplifies it to its original strength and then again forwards it to the destination. Basically, repeaters are used in a network so that a signal can travel longer distance.

34. When the computer network uses telephone lines as communication channel, then MODEM is used as a data communication device. Now, explain the working of MODEM.

Ans. MODEM performs the task of modulation at sender's site and demodulation at the receiver's site. Basically, our computer generates data in the form of digital signals which need to be forwarded to the receiver through telephone lines. Since, telephone lines can carry only analog signals. So, digital signals need to be converted to analog signals at sender's site this is called **modulation**. At receiver's site, again analog signals should be converted back to the original digital signals, then this is called **demodulation**.

35. Difference between circuit switching and packet switching.

Ans. Differences between circuit switching and packet switching are as follows

Circuit Switching	Packet Switching
Initially designed for voice communication.	Initially designed for data transmission.
Inflexible, because once a path is set all parts of a transmission follows the same path.	Flexible, because a route is created for each packet to travel to the destination.
It is connection oriented.	It is connectionless.

36. Elucidate the following terms.

(i) PAN (ii) WiMAX (iii) Satellite

Ans. (i) **PAN** It stands for Personal Area Network. It is a computer network used for communication among computer and different technological devices close to it.

(ii) **WiMAX** It stands for Worldwide Interoperability for Microwave Access. It is a wireless transmission of data using a variety of transmission modes.

(iii) **Satellite** which are orbiting around the Earth, provide necessary links for telephone and television service.

37. Why do we use Instant Messaging?

Ans. Instant messaging is a set of communication technologies used for text based communication between two or more participants over the Internet or other types of networks. Many instant messaging services offer video calling features, Voice over Internet Protocol (VoIP) and web conferencing services. Web conferencing services can integrate both video calling and instant messaging abilities.

38. How can you prepare for emergencies?

Ans. To prepare for emergencies, follow the given guidelines

(i) Follow workspace protocol and guidelines to ensure safety and health; know and understand rules and procedures concerning fire emergencies.

(ii) Ensure that smoke alarms and sprinkler systems are installed, working properly and are not blocked.

(iii) Conduct regular fire drills.

39. Explain any three rules that companies follows in terms of fire safety.

Ans. Any four rules that companies follows in terms of fire safety are as follows

(i) All fire alarms systems are working.

(ii) All fire escapes can be opened easily.

(iii) Automatic fire doors close correctly.

40. Explain three conditions following which evacuation is done.

Ans. Any three conditions following which evacuation is done are

- In the event of a fire, an immediate evacuation is to be followed by the employees.
- In case of tornadoes, earthquakes, floods or explosions, the type of building can be a major factor in taking decision to follow the evacuation plan.

- If a designated person within your workplace, under some circumstances had taken the decision to evacuate or shut down operations.

41. What are biological hazards?

Ans. Biological hazards are caused by bacteria, viruses, insects, plants, birds, animals and humans, etc. It includes exposure to harm or disease associated with working with animals, people or infectious plant materials. Workplaces like schools, day care, colleges, hospitals, laboratories or various outdoor establishments are more exposed to such type of biological hazards.

42. How does dry chemical fire extinguisher work?

Ans. Dry chemical fire extinguishers extinguish the fire primarily by interrupting the chemical reaction of the fire triangle. Today's most widely used type of fire extinguisher is the multipurpose dry chemical that is effective on Class A, B and C fires. This agent also works by creating a barrier between the oxygen element and the fuel element on Class A fires.

Ordinary dry chemical is for Class B and C fires only. It is important to use the correct extinguisher for the type of fuel. Using the incorrect agent can allow the fire to re-ignite after apparently being extinguished successfully.

• Long Answer Type Questions

43. Why is Internet called 'Network of Networks'?

Ans. Internet is called 'Network of Networks' because it is global network of computers that are linked together by cables and telephone lines making communication possible among them. It can be defined as a global network over a million of smaller heterogeneous computer networks.

The network which consists of thousands of networks spanning the entire globe is known as Internet. The Internet is a world wide collection of networked computers, which are able to exchange information with each other very quickly. Mostly people use the Internet in two ways, E-mail and World Wide Web. In Internet, most computers are not connected directly, they are connected to smaller networks, which in turn are connected through gateways to the Internet backbone. A gateway is a device that connects dissimilar networks. A backbone is central interconnecting structure - that connects one or more networks.

44. Give an example of E-mail address and explain each part of it.

Ans. The example of an E-mail address is abc@gmail.com. The format of E-mail address is username@hostname or domain name. So, as per the above example of E-mail address. abc is the username and gmail.com is the name of hosting server or host (domain) name. Thus, we can say that, E-mail address has two parts separated by '@' symbol.

(i) **Username** On the left side of separator @ is the user name. A user name cannot have blanks.

(ii) **Domain Name for the Host Server** The portion to the right of @ identifies the server or host network that services your E-mail. It is also known as E-mail server.

45. What do you mean by Instant Messaging? Also, explain one Instant Messaging software. **[CBSE Textbook]**

Ans. **Instant Messaging (IM)**, form of text-based communication in which two persons participate in a single conversation over their computers or mobile devices within an Internet based chatroom.

Various softwares provide instant messaging services as Whatsapp, Google Talk, Skype, Meebo, eBuddy, etc.

Google Talk It is an instant messaging and VoIP service developed by Google. This client lets you to log in to the service to chat and hold video-conferences with your friends from the windows desktop. Google Talk is more than just a regular chat, you can also make free PC to PC VoIP calls and even leave voice messages like an answering machine. If your contacts are also using the Google Hangouts client, you can send files too.

Google Hangouts was integrated into G-mail where users could send instant messages to other G-mail users. As it worked within a browser, the Google Talk client did not need to be downloaded to send instant messages to G-mail users.

46. What is switching? Explain the different types of switching techniques.

Ans. Switching is a technique which is used in large networks. It is a hardware or software device which creates a connection between one or more computers.

Switching is basically of three types which are as follows

(i) **Circuit Switching** In this type of technique, an end-to-end path is created before sending the data (dedicated channel, i.e. Circuit). The data is transferred using physical connection which is set upto between sender and receiver.

(ii) **Message Switching** Message switching is based on the transfer of block of messages from sender to receiver. Firstly, the address of destination is attached in a message. When a sender has a block of data to be sent, it is stored in the first switching station and then forwarded later. Each block of message is received entirely, checked for errors and then retransmitted.

There is no need for physical connection between packet which has header that contains source and destination addresses information acknowledgement and error bits.

(iii) **Packet Switching** In packet-based networks, the message gets broken into small data packets. These packets are sent out from the computer and they travel around the network seeking out the most efficient route to travel as circuits become available.

47. What is a topology? Explain the types of topologies.

Ans. Topology refers to the topology of a network. Topology refers to the way in which a network is laid out physically.

Topology is the geometric representation of the relationship of all the nodes to the one another. There are mainly four types of topologies as discussed below

(i) **Mesh Topology** In mesh topology, each computer is connected to every other computer to provide an alternate path for transferring data.

(ii) **Star Topology** In a star topology, each computer is connected to a centrally located device called hub.

(iii) **Bus Topology** In a bus topology, one long cable acts as a backbone to link all the computers in a network.

(iv) **Ring Topology** In a ring topology, each computer is connected with the two computers on either side of it.

48. What are the preventive measures to avoid cyberbullying?

Ans. Preventive measures to be taken to avoid cyberbullying are given as

(i) Check your privacy settings in social media like Facebook, so that your friends can only view your profile and posts.

(ii) You should think twice while posting any message, as internet is public.

(iii) Always keep your personal information like name, address, phone number, school name, credit card or debit card credentials, password, etc., private.

49. What are some examples of workplace hazards?

Ans. Some examples of workplace hazards are as follows:

(i) Damaged electrical outlets, cords, cables, etc.

(ii) Overloaded outlets and circuits.

(iii) Combustible substances in unsecured locations, (including excessive trash and recycling) - keep these far from electrical equipment.

(iv) Fire exit obstacles.

Keep workspace and equipment clean, dry and well-ventilated and especially clean of oil and dust.

50. What is the first aid you should apply for burns?

Ans. If you suspect that someone has a third-degree bum, call the hospital for ambulance. Seek professional medical care for any bums that

(i) Cover a large area of skin.

(ii) Are located on the person's face, groin, buttocks, hands or feet.

(iii) Have been caught by contact with chemicals or electricity.

To treat a minor burn, run cool water over the affected area for up to 15 min. If that's not possible, apply a cool compress to the area instead. Avoid applying ice to burned tissue, it can cause more damage.

Over-the-counter pain relievers can help relieve pain.

51. What is a workplace emergency?

Ans. A workplace emergency is an unforeseen situation that threatens your employees, customers or the public;disrupts or shuts down the workplace operations; or causes physical or environmental damage.

Emergencies may be natural or manmade and include the following

- Floods
- Hurricanes
- Fires
- Tornadoes
- Toxic gas releases
- Chemical spills
- Radiological accidents
- Explosions
- Civil disturbances
- Workplace violence resulting in bodily harm and trauma

52. Write any five precautions that are to be taken at the workplace.

Ans. Any five precautions that are to be taken of at the workplace are as follows:

(i) Take responsibility and clean up, if you made a mess.

(ii) Clean and organise your workspace.

(iii) Ensure a clear and easy route to emergency exits and equipment.

(iv) Be alert and awake on the job.

(v) Be attentive at all times to your work surroundings.

53. Explain the concept 'Watch Your Plate' to maintain a healthy body at workplace.

Ans. The explanation of the concept 'Watch Your Plate' to maintain a healthy body at workplace is

(i) Promote consumption of a variety of foods and awareness regarding their serving sizes.

(ii) Encourage conscious calorie reduction.

(iii) Make available fresh vegetables and fruits in the cafeteria.

(iv) Make clean water the default drink in the workplace and at meetings and discourage sugar-sweetened beverages.

(v) Discourage consumption of foods high in salt, sugar and saturated and transfats.

54. Explain some of the ways to remove workplace hazards.

Ans. Some of the ways to eliminate workplace hazards are as follows

(i) Remove damaged electrical outlets, cords, cables, etc.

(ii) Check overloaded outlets and circuits.

(iii) Combustible substances in unsecured locations, (including excessive trash and recycling) - keep these far from electrical equipment.

(iv) Clear all fire exit obstacles.

(v) Keep workspace and equipment clean, dry and well-ventilated and especially clean of oil and dust.

(vi) Follow workspace protocol and guidelines to ensure safety and health; know and understand rules and procedures concerning fire emergencies.

(vii) Ensure that smoke alarms and sprinkler systems are installed, working properly and are not blocked.

(viii) Conduct regular fire drills.

55. Explain some of the actions that are used in the event of fire.

Ans. Some actions that should be used in the event of a fire are as follows:

(i) Close all the windows, doors and switch of non-essential services.

(ii) Walk to the nearest assembly point.

(iii) Follow the emergency signs.

(iv) Escape routes should be lit by emergency lighting so that people can use them safely if an emergency occurs.

(v) Don't re-enter the building until permission is given by the person in charge of the evacuation.

(vi) If the fire is small, but only if you are trained to do so use fire extinguishers to attempt to put the fire out.

56. Explain any five precautions at workplace.

Ans. Any five precautions at workplace are as follows:

(i) First aid boxes at various places in the office.

(ii) Trained first aiders - on all floors of a building.

(iii) Knowledge of the nearest casualty department or local hospital.

(iv) Access to call for an ambulance.

(v) Ability to provide immediate assistance to casualties with illnesses or injuries caused by a specific hazard at work.

57. Explain how to apply roller bandage to a wound.

Ans. To apply a roller bandage to a wound, follow these steps:

(i) Hold the injured area steady.

(ii) Gently but firmly wrap the bandage around the injured limb or body part, covering the wound.

(iii) Fasten the bandage with sticky tape or safety pins.

(iv) The bandage should be wrapped firmly enough to stay put, but not so tightly that it cuts off blood flow.

To check the circulation in a bandaged limb, pinch one of the person's fingernails or toenails until the color drains from the nail. If color do not return within two seconds of letting go, the bandage is too tight and needs to be adjusted.

58. Explain any five moves that an employee can do on hearing the fire alarm.

Ans. On hearing the fire alarm, the employees should

(i) Close all the windows, doors and switch of non-essential services.

(ii) Walk to the nearest assembly point.

(iii) Follow the emergency signs.

(iv) Escape routes should be lit by emergency lighting, so that people can use them safely if an emergency occurs.

(v) Don't re-enter the building until permission is given by the person in charge of the evacuation.

59. How does keeping a watch at the stress level can help to sustain in the workplace?

Ans. (i) Introduce stress consultation and counselling services for staff.

(ii) Create a physical space for reflection and thinking.

(iii) Create a system to reinforce a healthy, positive and balanced workplace.

(iv) Promote de-stressing (relaxation) exercise, e.g. yoga, tai-chi, deep breathing, meditation, etc.

(v) Create time and space for recreational activities at work.

(vi) Build social support groups.

Chapter Test

Multiple Choice Questions

1. A web page is located using a
(a) Universal Record Linking
(b) Uniform Resource Locator
(c) Universal Record Locator
(d) Uniformly Reachable Links

2. Instant messaging service accepts instant messages from
(a) external sites
(b) internal sites
(c) Both (a) and (b)
(d) None of these

3. Which of the following is an application based instant messaging software?
(a) Google Talk
(b) eBuddy
(c) Meebo
(d) MSN Web Messenger

4. A blog consists of
(a) images
(b) text
(c) links
(d) All of these

5. .... is the act of posting content on a blog.
(a) Edublog
(b) Posting
(c) Blogging
(d) Blogger

6. Which of the following offers a blog service?
(a) Drupal
(b) Joomla
(c) WordPress.com
(d) All of these

7. Qumana is an offline blog editor which is used for .... operating system(s).
(a) Windows
(b) Mac
(c) Both (a) and (b)
(d) None of these

8. Which of the following websites is used for booking train tickets?
(a) Nykaa
(b) IRCTC
(c) RedBus
(d) Myntra

Short Answer Type Questions

9. Write any two blog platforms with Qumana works.

10. Explain the purpose of online transactions.

11. List any five websites that allow online transactions.

12. What do you mean by Cash on Delivery?

Long Answer Type Questions

13. What are the differences between star topology and bus topology of network?

14. What are the benefits of online shopping?

15. What is a computer network? Why do we need networking in our system?

16. What are the preventive measures to avoid phishing and spamming?

17. Explain the different types of accidents.

Answers

Multiple Choice Questions

1. (b) *2. (a)* *3. (a)* *4. (d)* *5. (c)* *6. (d)* *7. (c)* *8. (b)*

For Detailed Solutions
Scan the code

Information Technology
Class 10th (Term II)

Practice Paper 1*
(Solved)

General Instructions

- **Time :** 2 Hours
- **Max. Marks :** 25

1. There are 8 questions in the question paper. All questions are compulsory.
2. Question no. 1 is a Case Based Question, which has five MCQs. Each question carries one mark.
3. Question no. 2-6 are Short Answer Type Questions. Each question carries 2 marks.
4. Question no. 7-8 are Long Answer Type Questions. Each question carries 5 marks.
5. There is no overall choice. However, internal choices have been provided in some questions. Students have to attempt only one of the alternatives in such questions.

**** As exact Blue-print and Pattern for CBSE Term II exams is not released yet. So the pattern of this paper is designed by the author on the basis of trend of past CBSE Papers. Students are advised not to consider the pattern of this paper as official, it is just for practice purpose.***

1. Direction *Read the following passage and answer the questions that follows*

Netiquette is a combination of the words network and etiquette and is defined as a set of rules for acceptable online behaviour. Similarly, online ethics focuses on the acceptable use of online resources in an online social environment. Netiquette exists to help people to communicate more effectively whilst online, and to avoid unnecessary misunderstandings and potential conflicts. Without a sound understanding of netiquette you run the risk of displaying abusive or cyber bullying type behaviour without even being aware of it. Netiquette is a new word and concept for some of us, but a basic understanding of netiquette is important for everybody that uses the internet.

(i) Netiquette is short for
(a) internet etiquette
(b) net etiquette
(c) net quitte
(d) None of these

(ii) Which of the following is/are rule(s) for netiquette?
(a) Respect people's privacy
(b) Don't be sarcastic
(c) Respect other's views
(d) All of these

(iii) Netiquette includes several aspects of Internet such as ....
(a) e-mail
(b) social media
(c) outline chat
(d) All of these

(iv) Avoid posting ....comments online.
(a) offensive
(b) polite
(c) respectfully
(d) All of these

(v) ....other when you are new.
(a) Always truth
(b) Do not trust
(c) Sometimes trust
(d) None of these

2. What do you mean by the term computer accessibility? What are the different types of disabilities that affect the usage of computer?

Or What should a person do on hearing the fire alarm at workplace?

3. State the advantages of a database.

Or Explain the workplace hazards in terms of uncontrolled energy.

4. Define the terms field, record and file.

5. Explain the advantages of networking.

Or Define the following terms

(i) Switch (ii) Hub

6. Why do we use Instant Messaging?

Or Write the steps to create a new post in Qumana.

7. What are the myths about entrepreneurship?

Or Explain the role of an entrepreneur as an enterprising man and the person who reinvents organisation.

8. Explain DDL and TCL in terms of database.

Or What is table? Define candidate key. Differentiate between the primary key and alternate key.

Explanations

1. (i) (*a*) Netiquette is short for Internet etiquette. It states a number of rules that should be followed while working online.

(ii) (*d*) A person working online should follow some rules like one should be open to understand the views of others. People should not infringe the privacy of other person and behave properly without being abusive.

(iii) (*d*) E-mail, social media and outline chat are only possible using Internet and thus netiquettes should be followed while working on these platforms.

(iv) (*a*) One should avoid posting/commenting any abusive or offensive statement which can hurt other's sentiments.

(v) (*b*) While online, one should not trust anyone as no one knows anyone face-to-face. The ones whom you personally know can be trusted upto a little extent.

2. Computer accessibility refers to customizing the functioning of the computer parts. These accessibility options enables people with a disability or impairment to use a computer.

The different types of disabilities that affect the usage of computer are as follows

- Eyesight like low vision, color blindness, etc.
- Dexterity like paralysis of any body part like arms, hands or fingers injured.
- Hearing like deafness.
- Speech impairment (difficulty in understanding).
- Reasoning like learning disability (dyslexia) or difficulty to concentrate.

Or

A person should perform the following steps on hearing the fire alarm at workplace

- Close all the windows, doors and switch of non-essential services.
- Walk to the nearest assembly point.
- Follow the emergency signs.
- Escape routes should be lit by emergency lighting so that people can use them safely if an emergency occurs.
- Don't re-enter the building until permission is given by the person in charge of the evacuation.
- If the fire is small, but only if you are trained to do so use fire extinguishers to attempt to put the fire out.

3. The advantages of a database are as follows

Sharing of Data Different users can use the same database to access the data according to their needs.

Avoids data Redundancy Data redundancy means duplication of data. It avoids duplication of data and ensures that there is only one instance of certain data.

Highly Securable Database can be secured by assigning a lock to it by using keys.

Confidentiality The DBMS can ensure different views for the different users of the database. This keeps the confidentiality of the data safe.

Or

The workplace hazards in terms of uncontrolled energy are as follows

- An object that could fall from a height (potential or gravitational energy),

- A run-away chemical reaction (chemical energy),
- The release of compressed gas or steam (pressure; high temperature),
- Entanglement of hair or clothing in rotating equipment (kinetic energy), or
- Contact with electrodes of a battery or capacitor (electrical energy).

4. **Fields** A column within a table that contains only one type of information is called a field. *For example*, Name, Address, Date of Birth and Phone Number are different field names.

   Record A set of various fields is called a record. All the information in the table in various columns represents a record. *For example*, the information entered under the fields, Name, Address, Date of Birth and Phone Number indicate the record of students.

   File A file is a collection of related records.

5. The advantages of networking are as follows:
   (i) **User Communication** Network allows users to communicate using emails, social networking sites, video conferencing, etc.
   (ii) **File Sharing** By using networking, data or information can be shared or transferred from one computer to another.
   (iii) **Media and Entertainment** Most of the companies and TV channels use network to broadcast audio and video including live radio and television programmes.
   (iv) **Hardware Sharing** Hardware components such as printers, scanners, etc. can also be shared. *For example*, instead of purchasing 10 printers, one printer can be purchased and shared among multiple users thus saving cost.

   Or

   (i) **Switch** A switch is a device which connects multiple communication lines together. It is used to create temporary connections between two or more devices linked to switch.
   (ii) **Hub** A hub is a central device in a network that provides common connection among the computers or nodes. It is used in star topology.

6. Instant messaging is a set of communication technologies used for text based communication between two or more participants over the Internet or other types of networks. Many instant messaging services offer video calling features, Voice over Internet Protocol (VoIP) and web conferencing services. Web conferencing services can integrate both video calling and instant messaging abilities.

   Or

   To create a new post in Qumana, follow the below steps
   (i) Click on New Post option. A window will appear.
   (ii) Type the title and content of the post in respective fields.
   (iii) Click on Publish Post button.

7. The myths about entrepreneurship are as follows
   (i) **It is easy to start a business** In reality, starting a successful business is a very difficult and challenging process. The rate of failure of new ventures is high. Even after a period of seven years, only one third of the enterprises are profitable. However, it is relatively easy to start a very small business than a large company.
   (ii) **Lots of money is needed to start a new business** A business can be started with limited money. For example, Infosys Technology was started with only ₹10,000. In the beginning you can hire space and equipment.
   (iii) **A startup cannot borrow from banks** Under various schemes like MUDRA, budding entrepreneurs also can raise loans from banks.
   (iv) **Talent is more important than industry** The nature of industry an entrepreneur chooses has a great effect on success and growth. For example, if you enter an industry wherein competition is cut throat or materials are scarce, you may fail.
   (v) **Most startups are successful** A large percentage of startups fail. The average profit of an owner managed firm is ₹20,000 per month. Very few entrepreneurs earn more than employees.

   Or

   Enterprising man A business does not get started by itself. It is the entrepreneur who takes the risks and is willing to face devastating failure. He braves uncertainty, strikes out on his own, and through native wit, devotion to duty, and singleness of purpose, somehow creates business and industrial activity where none existed before. His values and activities have become integral to corporate culture.

   Person who reinvents organisation An entrepreneur continuously works to reinvent his organisation. He knows that change is a constant in and around his organisation. They initiate changes. Paul Wilken observes, "Entrepreneurship is a discontinuous phenomenon, appearing to initiate changes in the production process and then disappearing until it reappears to initiate another change." Thus, entrepreneurs reinvent organisations by the spirit of change and danger.

8. **Data Definition Language (DDL)** This command enables you to perform the following tasks
   - Create, alter, and drop schema objects
   - Grant and revoke privileges and roles
   - Add comments to the data dictionary

   The CREATE, ALTER and DROP commands require exclusive access to the object being acted upon. For example, an ALTER TABLE command fails if another user has an open transaction on the specified table.

Transaction Control Language (TCL) Transaction control commands manage changes made by DML commands. These SQL commands are used for managing changes affecting the data. These commands are COMMIT, ROLLBACK and SAVEPOINT.

Or

A table consists of a number of rows and columns. Each record contains values for the attributes.

A candidate key is the smallest subset of the super key for which there does not exist a proper subset that is super key. Any candidate key can be chosen to uniquely identify the records, it is called primary key.

A primary key is a value that can be used to identify a unique row in a table. While an alternate key is any candidate key which is not selected to be the primary key.

Example Consider table PERSON

Name	Bank A/c Num	Aadhar Num
Shanu	12908809	10991222
Gopal	19090909	19089090
Bhavish	19020909	829821282

So, Bank A/c Num and Aadhar Num are the candidate keys for the table.

Primary Key Aadhar Num

Alternate Key Bank A/c Num

Information Technology
Class 10th (Term II)

Practice Paper 2*
(Solved)

General Instructions

- **Time :** 2 Hours
- **Max. Marks :** 25

1. There are 8 questions in the question paper. All questions are compulsory.
2. Question no. 1 is a Case Based Question, which has five MCQs. Each question carries one mark.
3. Question no. 2-6 are Short Answer Type Questions. Each question carries 2 marks.
4. Question no. 7-8 are Long Answer Type Questions. Each question carries 5 marks.
5. There is no overall choice. However, internal choices have been provided in some questions. Students have to attempt only one of the alternatives in such questions.

As exact Blue-print and Pattern for CBSE Term II exams is not released yet. So the pattern of this paper is designed by the author on the basis of trend of past CBSE Papers. Students are advised not to consider the pattern of this paper as official, it is just for practice purpose.

1. Direction *Read the following passage and answer the questions that follows*

A web browser is a piece of software that enables the user to access web pages and web applications on the internet. There is a range of browsers available, and they are usually free to download and install. It acts as an interface between server and user, and displays web documents to the client. The web browser sends an HTTP request and gets an HTTP response. Mozilla Firefox, Google Chrome, Internet Explorer, etc are some examples of the web browsers. The primary function of a web browser is to display HTML code which helps in designing the web page. Each time a browser loads a web page, it processes the HTML, including text, links, and references to images and other items, like CSS and JavaScript functions. The web browser processes these items, and displays them on the browser window.

(i) Which of the following is a piece of software?
(a) Web browser (b) Web interface
(c) Web server (d) Internet

(ii) Between which of the following a web browser acts as an interface?
(a) Browser and user
(b) Server and User
(c) Javascript and Google
(d) HTML and CSS

(iii) Which of the following is not a web browser?
(a) Mozilla Firefox (b) Google Chrome
(c) Internet Explorer (d) Microsoft Frontpage

(iv) Each time a browser loads a web page, it processes the
(a) Style sheet (b) HTTP request
(c) HTML (d) HTTP response

(v) CSS stands for

(a) Casting Style Sheet (b) Control Style Sheet
(c) Client Style Sheet (d) Cascading Style Sheet

2. What is instant messaging? Mention some of the key features of an instant messaging software.

Or Explain the Text, Memo and Auto Number data types in Access.

3. Explain the biological and chemical hazards caused in workplace.

4. State the types of relationship in database tables.

Or State any three advantages of database.

5. Explain any two types of networks.

Or What is E-commerce? State some of the popular online transaction websites.

6. Identify the following devices

(i) A device that is used to connect different types of networks. It performs the necessary translation, so that the connected networks can communicate properly.

(ii) A device that converts data from digital bit stream into an analog signal and *vice-versa*.

Or Mr. Lal owns a factory which manufactures automobile spare parts. Suggest him the advantages of having a web page for his factory.

7. What is sustainable development? State the main principles of sustainable development.

Or Explain the short-term solutions related to sustainable development.

8. Mention some of the major advantages of Internet.

Or What is the use of ease of access option in control panel? Explain the options available in it.

Explanations

1. (i) (*a*) Web browser is a piece of software. It is an application program used to access the www. It works as a gateway to the world of internet.

(ii) (*b*) A web browser acts as an interface between the user and the server. Using the web browser, a user enter the data to be searched/retrieved and the server sends the required information.

(iii) (*d*) Microsoft is not a web browser but a discontinued WYSIWYG HTML editor.

(iv) (*c*) Each time a browser loads a web page, it processes the HTML code. The browser fetches the data as required by the user by processing the HTML code that runs at the backend of any request made by the user.

(v) (*d*) Cascading Style Sheet is a style sheet language used for describing the presentation of a document written in a markup language such as HTML. CSS is a cornerstone technology of the World Wide Web, alongside HTML and JavaScript.

2. **Instant Messaging (IM)** is a form of communication over the Internet that offers an instantaneous transmission of text-based messages from sender to receiver.

To use instant messaging software, a user must have a valid messaging account. Some key features of an instant messaging software are as follows

(i) Sending text-messages to more than one person at same time
(ii) Audio and video calling
(iii) Audio and video conferencing
(iv) Messages History for future reference
(v) Transferring of files

Or

Text Data is the data used to 'store' Text or a combination of Text and Numbers which do not 'require calculations'.

For example, Roll Numbers/Names of Students.

Memo Data is used for storing elaborate and lengthy Text data.

For example, A line or remark written about each student.

Auto Number Data is used to generate a running series of numbers which can be used to uniquely identify the records of a table and can act as the primary key if required.

For example, Roll numbers of students.

3. The biological and chemical hazards caused in workplace are as follows

Biological hazards caused by bacteria, viruses, insects, plants, birds, animals, and humans, etc. It includes exposure to harm or disease associated with working with animals people or infectious plant materials. Workplaces like schools, day care, colleges, hospitals, laboratories, or various outdoor establishments are more exposed to such type of biological hazards.

Chemical hazard It depends on the physical, chemical and toxic properties of the chemical in any form (solid, liquid or gaseous). This type of hazards can cause skin irritation, illness or breathing problems.

4. There are three main types of relationships that can be created between the tables in an access database. They are: One-to-one Relationships

In a one-to-one relationship, one record in a table is associated with one and only one record in another table.

One-to-many Relationships

In a one-to-many relationship, one record in a table can be associated with one or more records in another table.

Many-to-many Relationships

A many-to-many relationship occurs when multiple records in a table are associated with multiple records in another table.

Or

Any three advantages of database are as follows

(i) **Facilitate Sharing of Data** Multiple users can pick the same piece of data at the same time, from a centrally stored database, and use it for different purposes. A database also allows the same piece of data to be shared by multiple applications at the same time.

(ii) **Prevent Duplication of Data** As all the data in a database is stored at one place which is centrally located, there are slim chances of data entry getting repeated or duplicated.

(iii) **Ensure Data Consistency** Data consistency is ensured in a database because there is no duplication of data. All data appears consistently across the database and the data is same for all the users viewing the database. Moreover, any changes made to the database are immediately reflected to all the users and there is no data inconsistency.

5. The two types of networks are as follows

(i) **Local Area Network** A Local Area Network (LAN) is the one which connects computers and devices in a limited geographical area such as home, school, office or any closely placed group of buildings. It provides very high speed. Usually, LANs are used for connecting computers and peripherals such as printers, scanners, etc.

(ii) **Metropolitan Area Network** A Metropolitan Area Network (MAN) is a computer network in which two or more computers which are geographically distributed but in the same metropolitan city. Its geographic scope falls between a WAN and LAN.

Or

E-Commerce is a major application of Internet. Users can buy or sell goods over the Internet by paying online using a credit card or debit card.

Some of the popular online transaction websites are as follows

(i) **IRCTC** An online portal for booking and cancellation of train tickets.

(ii) **Flipkart** An online shopping portal for buying products.

(iii) **Ebay** An online shopping portal for buying and selling goods.

(iv) **Redbus** An online portal for booking bus tickets.

6. (i) Router (ii) Modem

Or

The web page provides the information to the clients about his factory of spare parts. Moreover, he can receive the order on the Internet from the clients using the web page.

7. Sustainable development is the way to reach development without causing a harm or damage to the environment. Sustainable development has three dimensions ecological, economic and social. Achievement of sustainable development requires the integration of economic, environmental, and social components at all levels.

Main principles of sustainable development are as follows

(i) Respect and care for all forms of life.

(ii) Improving the quality of human life.

(iii) Minimising the depletion of natural resources.

(iv) Conserving the earth's vitality and diversity.

(v) Enabling communities to care for their own environment.

(vi) Changing personal attitude and practices towards the environment.

Or

The short-term solutions related to sustainable development are as follows

(i) Illegal deforestation and smuggling of forest resources and minerals should be stopped.

(ii) People should be encouraged to regenerate forest, quantitatively and qualitatively, to compensate for the loss of forest cover.

(iii) During legal deforestation, a proper balance ought to be maintained between deforestation and afforestation.

(iv) Waste and sewage discharge into water bodies is one of the chief causes of pollution. Hence, proper treatment system, recycling of waste, and their proper disposal should be undertaken.

(v) Planning and building exclusive industrial zones to manage and process all types of wastes.

(vi) Polluting industries should be relocated to outskirts of cities, far away from residential areas.

(vii) Prohibition of toxic chemical consumption can be vital for improving quality of arable land. Less chemical fertilizers should be used along with environment-friendly pesticides and weedicide.

8. Some of the major advantages of the internet are as follows

(i) **E-mail** E-mail is an online correspondence system. With e-mail you can send and receive instant electronic messages, which works like writing letters.

(ii) **Access Information** The Internet is a virtual treasure trove of information. The 'search engines' on the Internet can help you to find data on any subject that you need.

(iii) **Shopping** Along with getting information on the Internet, you can also shop online. There are many online stores and sites that can be used to look for products as well as buy them using your credit card.

(iv) **Online Chat** There are many 'chat rooms' on the web that can be accessed to meet new people, make new friends, as well as to stay in touch with old friends.

(v) **Downloading Software** You can download innumerable, games, music, videos, movies, and a host of other entertainment software from the Internet, most of which are free.

Or

Ease of access center is a central location where you can change accessibility options to make a computer easier to see, hear and use. It allows you to set up tools and change options by clicking links that address common needs.

Ease of access center opens, and the four choices in are highlighted one by one.

The different options available are as follows

- Narrator, a basic screen reader, reads the content aloud as it is highlighted and describes the on-screen activity. It is useful for people with hearing impairment.
- Magnifier, to magnify text and visuals for people with less eye sight.
- On screen keyboard with sticky keys and filter keys for people who have problem with motor skills or hand movement.
- Set up high contrast on screen to optimize visual displays or make them clearer.

Information Technology
Class 10th (Term II)

Practice Paper 3*
(Solved)

General Instructions

- **Time :** 2 Hours
- **Max. Marks :** 25

1. There are 8 questions in the question paper. All questions are compulsory.
2. Question no. 1 is a Case Based Question, which has five MCQs. Each question carries one mark.
3. Question no. 2-6 are Short Answer Type Questions. Each question carries 2 marks.
4. Question no. 7-8 are Long Answer Type Questions. Each question carries 5 marks.
5. There is no overall choice. However, internal choices have been provided in some questions. Students have to attempt only one of the alternatives in such questions.

***** As exact Blue-print and Pattern for CBSE Term II exams is not released yet. So the pattern of this paper is designed by the author on the basis of trend of past CBSE Papers. Students are advised not to consider the pattern of this paper as official, it is just for practice purpose.***

1. Direction *Read the following passage and answer the questions that follows*

Consider the following SQL command to create a table:

```
CREATE TABLE MEMBER
( MEM_ID INTEGER NOT NULL,
NAME CHAR(15) NOT NULL,
DATE_JOIN DATE,
ADDRESS VARCHAR(100) NOT NULL,
PH_NO CHAR(15),
);
```

(i) NOT NULL ensures that
(a) Column cannot have blank value (b) Column will not accept any value
(c) Column has a fixed value (d) Column has a unique value

(ii) By default format of date entered is
(a) DD-MM-YY (b) MM-DD-YY
(c) YYY-MM-DD (d) DD-MM-YYYY

(iii) The ……… constraint ensures that the value entered specifies a certain condition.
(a) NOT NULL (b) NULL
(c) CHECK (d) All of these

(iv) PRIMARY KEY in above example ensures that
   (a) MEM_ID is entered primarily
   (b) MEM_ ID will hold a uniquely identified value
   (c) MEM_ ID will not remain blank
   (d) All of these

(v) Which SQL command is used to create a table?
   (a) ALTER (b) INSERT
   (c) UPDATE (d) CREATE

2. State any three rules and netiquettes while chatting.

Or How does water and foam, and carbon dioxide work to extinguish fire?

3. Explain the three types of switching techniques.

Or Explain any one accident that may happen in workplace.

4. What is DML and DCL?

5. What are the best practices to be followed for internet security?

Or Define the terms network layout and topology. Explain any three network topologies.

6. Damini is a programmer in an institute and is asked to handle the records containing information of students. Suggest any 5 fields name and their data type of students database.

Or Write a SQL command to create the table BANK whose structure is given below.

Table : BANK

Field Name	Datatype	Size	Constraint
ID__Number	integer	10	Primary key
Name	varchar	20	
B_date	date		
Address	varchar	50	

7. Explain the functions of an entrepreneur.

Or Explain the advantages of choosing entrepreneurship as a career option.

8. Explain the features of database.

Or What is database, relational database and RDBMS?

Explanations

1. (i) (*a*) By default column holds NULL value. To change it and not let the value to stored as blank, NOT NULL constraint is used.

   (ii) (*c*) For date related data MySQL has three data types- DATE, DATETIME and TIMESTAMP.

   (iii) (*c*) The CHECK constraint ensures that all values in a column satisfy certain condition. It is used for quality control.

   (iv) (b) PRIMARY KEY constraint is used to uniquely identify each row in a table.

   (v) (*d*) The CREATE command is used to create the structure of a table. The syntax to create a table is:

   CREATE table <Table name>
   {
   <Data type> <Field Name1>,
   <Data type> <Field Name2>,
   <Data type> <Field Name3>
   };

2. Any three rules and netiquettes while chatting are as follows
   (i) **Do Not Use All Caps** Typing your message in UPPERCASE is like shouting on the Internet and very aggressive.
   (ii) **Give People Time to Respond** Be polite while online. If you are chatting with your friend, do not ask multiple questions in a short time, so that the recipient has time to respond.
   (iii) **Respect Others while Chatting** Give the person you are communicating with your undivided attention.

Or

Water and foam fire extinguishers extinguish the fire by taking the heat element away from the fire. Water extinguishers are for class A fires only – they should not be used on class B or C fires.

Carbon dioxide fire extinguishers extinguish fire by taking away the oxygen element of the fire triangle and also be removing the heat with a very cold discharge.

Carbon dioxide can be used on Class B and C fires. They are usually ineffective on Class A fires.

3. Switching is basically of three types which are as follows
   (i) **Circuit Switching** In this type of technique, an end-to-end path is created before sending the data (dedicated channel, i.e. Circuit). The data is transferred using physical connection which is set up between sender and receiver.
   (ii) **Message Switching** Message switching is based on the transfer of block of messages from sender to receiver. Firstly, the address of destination is attached in a message. When a sender has a block of data to be sent, it is stored in the first switching station and then forwarded later. Each block of message is received entirely, checked for errors and then retransmitted. There is no need for any physical connection between the source and destination.
   (iii) **Packet Switching** In this type of switching, a message is broken into packets of fixed size. Each packet has header that contains source and destination addresses information, acknowledgement and error bits.

Or

Any one accident that may happen in workplace is as follow

Slips, trips and falls One of the common accidents in workplace is slipping on wet floor or you likely encountered slippery tiled surfaces. Other risks are falling from height while working, falling from stairs and scaffolding. These accidents can happen in any work environment and the injuries sustained can range in severity. If a person were injured in the course of work as the result of a slip and fall or other type of accident, he/she may be entitled to financial support in the form of workers' compensation or Social Security disability.

4. **Data Manipulation Language (DML)** are the SQL commands are used for storing, retrieving, modifying, and deleting data. These commands are SELECT, INSERT, UPDATE, and DELETE. A Data Manipulation Language (DML) is a family of syntax elements similar to a computer programming language used for selecting, inserting, deleting and updating data in a database. Performing read-only queries of data is sometimes also considered a component of DML.

Data Control Language (DCL) is used to create roles, permissions, and referential integrity as well it is used to control access to the database by securing it. These SQL commands are used for providing security to database objects. These commands are GRANT and REVOKE.

5. The best practices to be followed for Internet security are as follows
   (i) **Do Not Share Personal Information** Never share your personal information while filling online forms.
   (ii) **Secure Transactions** Be careful while doing transactions on the Internet. Your account details, credit card number or online banking personal information can be tracked and used by unauthorised users known as hackers. Make sure, the website is legitimate.
   (iii) **Install Firewalls** Firewall acts as a bridge between your computer and other systems from which you are getting data.
   (iv) **Never Install Software from Unknown Sources** Verify the source or website while downloading any product or software.

Or

The arrangement of connected nodes (Computers) in a communicating network is called Network Layout.

Topology refers to the way in which a network is laid out physically. It is the geometric representation of the relationship of all the nodes to one another.

Any three network topologies are as follows:

Star Topology: In a star topology, each computer is connected to a centrally located device called hub.

Bus Topology: In a bus topology, one long cable acts as a backbone to link all the computers in a network.

Ring Topology: In a ring topology, each computer is connected with the two computers on either side of it.

6.

Field Name	Data Type
RollNo	Number
Name	Text
Class	Text
Section	Text
Gender	Text

Or

The SQL command to create a table as per given structure is as follows

```
Mysql> CREATE TABLE BANK (ID__Number
integer (10) PRIMARY KEY, Name varchar
(20), B__date Date, Address varchar
(50));
```

7. The functions of an entrepreneur are as follows
   (i) **Innovation** It includes introducing new products, opening new markets, new sources of raw material, and new organisation structure.

   To arrange for factors of production and establishing coordination, i.e., land, labour, capital etc. in appropriate proportion and to maximise output by best utilisation of these factors after coordinating them.
   (ii) **Finding Suitable Market** He has to search for suitable market to sell the product, for which he performs various functions advertisement and publicity, appointment of selling agents, providing incentives to various selling intermediaries to promote sales.
   (iii) **New Inventions** Encouraging new inventions and introducing innovations in production, production techniques, sales, marketing, advertisement etc.
   (iv) **Establishing Relations with Government** To establish relations with government and its functionaries. In this regards his functions are obtaining licences, payment of taxes, selling the product to government and provision for export-import etc.

Or

The advantages of choosing entrepreneurship as a career option are as follows
   (i) **Independence** An entrepreneur is his own boss. He can take all decisions himself. He need not obey someone.
   (ii) **Ambition-Fulfilment** Some people want to convert their original ideas into a new product or service. *For example*, smart phone, electric vehicle, driver less train, etc.
   (iii) **Excitement** Entrepreneurship involves adventure. Some people resign their well paid jobs and launch their own venture due to excitement.
   (iv) **Freedom** Entrepreneurship allows the freedom to try out one's ideas. Freedom seeking people choose entrepreneurship as a career.
   (v) **Wealth Creation** Successful entrepreneurs create enormous wealth for themselves and their staff.

8. The features of database are as follows
   (i) **Datebase Management Software is Self Describing in Nature** All database software have a system catalog which stores description of database objects such as tables, views, synonyms, value ranges, indexes, user groups or users etc. This description about the data itself is called the metadata or data about data.
   (ii) **Program-data insulation or program-data independence** This feature allows us to change the structure of a database without affecting the DBMS programs that access data from the database.
   (iii) **Data abstraction** Database management systems hide complex data-structures and irrelevant details from the users. This simplifies the view of the data and makes it easier for the users to work on the database. This approach of database design is called data abstraction.
   (iv) **Support multiple views of the data** The database software allows each user to have their own view of the database which describes only the data that is of interest to that user or group of users.
   (v) **Backup and recovery facilities** Backup and recovery methods of database software allow users to protect data from any accidental loss. If a computer system fails in the middle of a complex update process, the recovery subsystem is responsible for making sure that the database is restored to its original state.

Or

A **database** is an integrated collection of logically related records or tables. A database consolidates records previously stored in separate files into a common pool of data records that provides data for many applications. The data is managed by software called database management systems (DBMS). The data stored in a database is independent of the application programs using it and of the types of secondary storage devices on which it is stored.

A **relational database** is a type of database where data is stored in one or more related tables, which makes it much simpler to query the database. Each table has a set of fields, which define the nature of the data stored in the table. A record is one instance of a set of fields in a table. To visualize this, think of the records as the rows of the table and the fields as the columns of the table.

The **Relational Database Management System** (RDBMS) is a type of Database Management System (DBMS) that allows us to create and work with the relational databases. Most RDBMS use SQL (Structured Query Language) as database query language. LibreOffice Base, Microsoft Access, and OpenOffice Base, Oracle, MySQL are examples of some popular Relational Database Management Systems.

9 789325 796690

Printed by Libri Plureos GmbH in Hamburg,
Germany